Nadia ELOUAER

Tax treatment of partial asset contributions under Tunisian law

Nadia ELOUAER

Tax treatment of partial asset contributions under Tunisian law

Commercial law, Business law

ScienciaScripts

This book is a translation from the original published under ISBN 978-613-8-39964-3.

Publisher:
Sciencia Scripts
is a trademark of
Dodo Books Indian Ocean Ltd. and OmniScriptum S.R.L publishing group

120 High Road, East Finchley, London, N2 9ED, United Kingdom
Str. Armeneasca 28/1, office 1, Chisinau MD-2012, Republic of Moldova, Europe
Printed at: see last page
ISBN: 978-620-6-23810-2

TABLE OF CONTENTS

GENERAL INTRODUCTION

In an economic era marked by fierce competition, companies must adopt all the methods authorized by law to improve their competitiveness and live up to the challenge of belonging to the global economic market.

To be competitive in an economy, you need to use all the modalities that are as effective as they are modern. To achieve this, companies need to have a certain level of financial and productive strength. To reach the required level of competitiveness, the company will sometimes have to modify its strategy, its capital structure, or quite simply, its investment policy. To achieve this, the company may choose to adopt one of the following corporate restructuring methods: merger, demerger or partial asset contribution.

What do these three concepts mean?

To define these concepts, we had to call on both commercial and tax law, while making it clear that these two disciplines do not present questionable divergences for the first two concepts.

The Tunisian Commercial Companies Code (CSC), promulgated by law no. 2000-93 of November 3, 2000, deals with the legal analysis of corporate restructuring and transformation operations in Book Five, entitled "Mergers, demergers, transformations and groupings of companies".

Article 411 of Title Two of the Code states that "a merger is the bringing together of two or more companies to form a single company". The formation of a new company may entail either the disappearance of the two merged companies; or, in the case of a merger-absorption, the disappearance of one of the two companies and the survival of the other.

In addition, demergers are defined in the same code in article 428 of title three on company demergers, which states: "A company is demerged by dividing its assets and liabilities between several existing companies or by creating new companies. The demerger may be total or partial. If the demerger is total, it *necessarily results in dissolution without liquidation of the demerged company"*.

The difference between a merger and a demerger lies essentially in the criterion of the liquidation of the company, which will transfer all its assets and liabilities to the beneficiary company.

However, the Tunisian legislator, in article 428 CSC, emphasizes the possibility of adopting a partial demerger, without further clarifying the contours of this notion. This raises the question of the legislator's negligence: is this omission deliberate?

In fact, an analysis of the CSC reveals that the notion of partial demerger was not the only one cited without an explicit definition. The CSC contains numerous loopholes that merit further consideration. Among the other notions cited by the said code, without having the merit of being analyzed in a more concise manner: the partial contribution of assets.

This third form of corporate restructuring has been parachuted in under article 319 of chapter two on commercial companies. This article states that "in the event of the merger of companies by absorption or the creation of a new company encompassing one or more of the pre-existing companies, as well as in the event of the partial contribution of assets by one company to another..." Through this article, the Tunisian legislator is content to enumerate this notion, but nothing more.

Doesn't the partial contribution of assets, which is not defined in the aforementioned code, merit a study to determine its scope, the procedure for setting it up and the consequences of adopting it?

In practice, companies - not only Tunisian ones - are increasingly adopting this restructuring method. But, in the absence of a legal definition, how can these companies justify their choices and the necessary implementation procedures?

In view of the importance of the partial contribution of assets in both economic and tax terms, it is appropriate to attempt to define this concept by going through the logic of defining the contribution to a company in general, and then to justify this choice by drawing on both French and European law.

A contribution is an asset or set of assets made available to the company by an associate, who may be a natural or legal person. The contribution may be in industry, in cash, in kind or even a partial contribution of assets.

Tax law associates the notion of contribution directly with the formation of a company. "Any incorporation necessarily implies the pooling of certain assets by the partners. These assets, which are made available to the company, are known as contributions. These contributions may consist of sums of money (cash contribution) or assets such as a building, a business, or a patent (contribution in kind), the ownership or enjoyment of which the partners transfer to the company in exchange for the delivery of shares subject to the company's contingencies[2] ".

If we compare the definition of a business contribution in commercial law with that in tax law, we can see that there is no divergence. However, it should be noted that, as already mentioned, this contribution to a company is diversified.

Contributions in industry, in kind, in cash and partial contributions of assets make up the whole of the contribution to the company.

A contribution in kind: this is the know-how that a person specializing in the field can contribute to guide the company's work. According to article 5 CSC,[3] , industrial contributions may not form part of a company's capital.

Cash contribution: this is a sum of money by which a natural or legal person participates in the capital of a company.

Contribution in kind: This is when an individual or legal entity contributes one or more items of real or personal property, tangible or intangible, by way of ownership or by way of enjoyment, to a company with the aim of becoming one of its partners or shareholders.

Partial asset contribution: Partial asset contribution is a concept that has no legal definition. Law no. 2000-93 of November 3, 2000, promulgating the CSC, is silent on the subject and offers no explanation.

On the other hand, according to Salah AMAMOU, a partial contribution of assets or a partial demerger occurs when the demerged company limits its contribution to the other companies to only part of its assets. In return, the company receives shares in the beneficiary companies, which are either retained in the portfolio (in which case the operation is referred to as a "partial contribution"), or immediately distributed among the shareholders. Whatever the destination of the securities received, however, the demerged or transferring company retains part of its assets and continues to exist, unlike in the case of a merger.[4]

By way of comparison, French law no. 66-537 of July 24, 1966 on commercial companies only deals with the transaction incidentally. Articles 387 and 388-1 of this law provide that joint-

---

[2] Revue Fiduciaire Group Dictionary, Paris 2003, page 80.
[3] Article 5 CSC: "... All of these contributions, with the exception of contributions in kind".
[4] Le manuel permanent du droit fiscal et du droit de douane tunisien, Amamou 1996, page 45.

4

stock companies and limited liability companies may subject a partial contribution of assets to the demerger regime. Under this law, the partial contribution of assets remains subject to the ordinary law governing contributions in kind.

On July 23 1990, the Council of the European Community adopted a directive[5] on the common system of taxation applicable to mergers, divisions, partial transfers of assets and exchanges of shares concerning companies of different Member States. The aim of this directive is to improve the conditions under which these operations are carried out, since they are of considerable importance in the economic relations between member states for the creation of the internal market.

Subsequently, Article 85 of the French Finance Act for 2002 provided for adjustments to the special regimes for corporate restructuring, and more specifically for mergers, demergers and partial asset contributions. These changes will be analyzed later.

It is clear that it is the tax system that has been dealt with both in the 1990 directive and in the Finance Act for 2002, while the very definition of the partial contribution of assets has only found its existence in doctrine.

A partial contribution of assets is a transaction whereby a legal entity contributes part of its assets to another legal entity and receives in exchange securities issued by the transferee company[6].

Referring to EU Directive 90/434/EEC of July 23, 1990 on the common system of taxation applicable to mergers, divisions, partial transfers of assets and exchanges of shares concerning companies of different Member States, the authors have deduced the following definition of a partial transfer of assets: "It is the complete branch of activity which comprises all the assets and liabilities of a division of a company which, from the organizational point of view, constitute an autonomous operation, i.e. a whole capable of functioning by its own means[7] ".

On the one hand, some authors find that: a partial contribution of assets is when a legal entity contributes part of its assets to the capital of another existing or newly-created entity, with a view to holding a share in the beneficiary company.

These definitions of partial asset contribution show that the purpose of the contribution is

[5] Official Journal of the European Communities of 20-08-1990, N°L225/1.
[6] OUDENOT Philippe: Fiscalité approfondie des sociétés, Paris, Litec 2001, page 694.
[7] De KERGOS Yann, RAFFIN Marie-Hélène and MARTIN Philippe: Fiscalité des fusions et apports partiels d'actifs, Paris, Litec, 1996

irrelevant to its classification. The partial contribution may relate to an isolated asset, to a set of heterogeneous assets, to a complete and autonomous branch of activity, or to all the assets of the contributing company.

On the other hand, Maurice COZIAN and Alain VIANDIER present the following definition: "A partial contribution of assets is a contribution in kind of an autonomous and complete branch of activity, made by a company called the contributor to a company called the beneficiary"[8] . We note that the definition adopted by Maurice COZIAN and Alain VIANDIER combines the notion of a contribution of assets in kind and the autonomous branch of activity, which seems logical given that the contributing company has the choice of participating in the capital of the beneficiary company either through one or all of its assets, or through one of its production divisions. In other words, the partial contribution of assets is a special type of contribution in kind, in the sense that it concerns an isolated asset or a division, a department, a homogeneous whole constituting a sub-company.

Indeed, these definitions are directly inspired by tax law solutions in this area. Whether in terms of corporate income tax or registration duties, the French General Tax Code allows the merger tax regime to be applied to the partial contribution of assets transaction, subject to the transfer of an entire autonomous branch of activity.

It should be noted that the benefit of this preferential regime, in the case of a partial contribution of assets not relating to an autonomous branch of activity, is conditional on obtaining ministerial approval. The concept of a branch of activity is regarded as a passport to exemption from approval.

The inclusion of the concept of an autonomous branch of activity in the definition of a partial transfer of assets requires clarification. As already mentioned, the European Community directive defines an autonomous branch of activity as all the assets and liabilities of a company which, from an organizational point of view, form a whole capable of functioning by its own means. In fact, the French tax authorities have adopted the European directive's definition of an autonomous branch of activity.

An analysis of the definition of "branch of activity" reveals a contradiction between the contribution in kind and this notion, which creates difficulties as to the precision of the partial contribution of assets.

---

[8] Juris-classeur société 1998 , fascicule 164-10

Firstly, as already defined, a contribution in kind is: "any property, movable or immovable, tangible or intangible (such as real estate, leasehold rights, goodwill, patents, receivables, etc.).

In accounting terms, a contribution in kind is only recognized as an asset on the balance sheet.

An autonomous branch of activity will contain assets such as a workshop, goodwill, production tools, receivables and customers. Symmetrically, this branch has commitments to its own suppliers and bankers.

Secondly, the contribution in kind must be integrated into the company so that it can generate future economic benefits. On its own, the company cannot carry out its business of producing goods and services.

A branch of activity is a division capable of operating autonomously and independently of the company (e.g. a packaging production department in a shoe manufacturing company), which is why it cannot be considered as an outright contribution in kind, but rather as a special type of contribution in kind.

Having attempted to define the partial contribution of assets, we now turn to an analysis of its characteristics. The partial contribution has two essential legal characteristics:

No dissolution of the transferring company.

The absence of a universal substitution effect.

1- *The absence of the dissolution of the sponsoring company:*

The dissolution of a company means the disappearance of its legal personality.

However, the fact that a company makes a partial contribution of assets does not mean that it disappears, since it retains the rest of its assets on the one hand, and its legal personality on the other: the partial contribution of assets does not result in the dissolution of the contributing company. It should be noted that even if the contribution includes all the industrial and/or financial assets of the contributing company, this does not change the legal nature of the transaction.

In this way, the transferring company becomes a partner or shareholder in the transferee. The shares issued by the transferee in return for the contribution take the place previously occupied by the contributed assets in the assets of the transferring company.

Unlike a merger-absorption, which results in the dissolution of the absorbed company, a partial contribution does not result in the dissolution of the contributing company.

2- *No universal substitution effect :*

From a legal point of view, a partial contribution constitutes a contribution in kind and does not therefore entail the universal transfer of the portion of assets and liabilities transferred.

As with any transaction carried out by economic agents, the partial contribution of assets must be in the interest of the author in the first instance, and of the economy in the second.

Initially, the partial asset contribution project can be adopted to create a joint subsidiary for two or more contributing companies. In this way, companies can adopt the partial contribution of assets as a cooperative technique to strengthen their position in an increasingly competitive market.

However, this strategic choice must not hinder free competition. Article 5 (new) of law no. 91-64 of July 29, 1991 on competition and prices[9] [10] as amended and supplemented by law no. 95-42 of April 24, 19959 : "Concerted actions and express or tacit agreements aimed at preventing, restricting or distorting competition on the market are prohibited when they are intended to:...

3- Restricting market access to other companies or the free exercise of competition;

4- Allocate markets or sources of supply..."

The adoption of this project by Tunisian companies, which are generally small and medium-sized enterprises, helps to reduce concentration in a sector of activity and encourages strategic alliances; However, this can only be done in compliance with the aforementioned law n°91-64, for fear of abusing the rule of law and hindering inter-firm competition. Companies may thus use this modality for reasons of control of competing companies, i.e. in this case there will be a limit to access to the market for the production of goods and services, consumer choice will be limited in this respect, and the national economy will be held by a few entrepreneurs, which may harm several areas of the national economy, such as the employment market.

Although the Tunisian legislator did not explicitly mention a specific regime or treatment for the partial contribution of assets as a corporate restructuring operation, he still retained the originality of implicitly adopting the treatment of this operation. According to the Tunisian legislator, mergers, demergers and partial contributions of assets are operations that are so close to each other that they can borrow rules from each other. For this reason, there are two chapters in the Tunisian Commercial Code, one dealing with mergers, the other with demergers. However, if we take this observation a step further, we can see that demerger operations refer the code user to the chapter on merger operations. Can this explicit reference to demergers justify the implicit reference

---

[9] Journal Officiel de la République Tunisienne N°55 du 6 Août 1991.
[10] Journal Officiel de la République tunisienne N°35 du 2 Mai 1995.

to the treatment of partial asset contributions, whether from a procedural or tax point of view, to the treatment of mergers? This reference is justified by the very close link that the legislator attributes to restructuring operations on the one hand, and the not yet widespread adoption of the partial contribution of assets within the managerial culture of Tunisian companies on the other.

Considering that these three restructuring operations are close to each other, the legislator has encouraged Tunisian entrepreneurs to increasingly adopt the operation that corresponds most closely to their strategic objectives. The partial contribution of assets can thus be considered as a means of encouraging investment.

Although the Tunisian legislator has not explicitly announced the treatment of partial asset contributions, he does recognize the existence of a specific regime for this operation. For its part, the Tunisian tax authorities, through their internal documentation and the various interpretations of the Commercial Companies Code and the various Finance Acts, have had occasion to interpret the analysis of this operation, although they do not often distinguish it from mergers and demergers.

The adoption of this form of corporate restructuring, i.e. the partial contribution of assets, automatically entails the transfer of the elements of the said contribution. This transfer is carried out according to precise legal procedures.

Given that the legal regime is adaptable to the nature of the adoption (contribution in kind or partial demerger), what tax treatment will apply to this restructuring operation?

Tunisian law, whether commercial or fiscal, does not react in a clear and explicit manner to this ambiguity. The Tunisian legislator, like his French counterpart, leaves it up to the two companies, the contributor and the beneficiary, to adopt the appropriate regime. However, the fact of leaving this room for manoeuvre, or of attributing a dual regime to the partial contribution of assets, does not affirm the existence of two axes of analysis.

Admittedly, a partial contribution of assets can be classified in two ways: as a special type of contribution in kind, or as a partial demerger. This dual classification does not jeopardize the originality of its treatment.

Like any legal rule, the tax treatment of this operation has a general application and special exceptions. But would the principle that the special prevails over the general be valid in the case of the tax treatment of this operation?

Legally, the special derogates from the general; in the case of the partial contribution of assets, this derogation is also special, since it is left to the goodwill of the two parties.

But, starting from this principle, the work plan throughout this book will be bilateral.

In the first part, the partial contribution of assets, whether in kind or partial demerger, goes through the necessary stages to determine the a priori taxable material that will serve as the basis for calculating a tax that must be liquidated within certain time limits set by the legislator. In this respect, the contribution will have a standard tax treatment that seems voluntary on the part of the Tunisian legislator, but will the truth be that this standard treatment is nothing more than a legislative loophole? (First part). In fact, if the Tunisian legislator has omitted this question even voluntarily, the Tunisian tax authorities, basing themselves on the almost total lack of texts on the subject, have been able to extract the originality of the tax treatment of this operation (second part) due to its implicit assimilation to merger operations.

Part I: Partial asset contribution: a voluntary standard treatment or a legislative loophole?

A partial contribution of assets is a transaction whereby a company contributes, without being dissolved, part of its assets and liabilities to another existing or newly-created company, in exchange for shares or equity interests in the capital of the beneficiary company.

The contribution may relate either to one or more isolated items, or to a set of assets making up a specific branch of activity.[11]

The parties to this contribution may decide by mutual agreement to subject the transaction to the special merger regime, or they may consider the partial asset contribution as a contribution in kind.

Indeed, the Tunisian Commercial Companies Code simply lists this category among the methods of increasing or forming the capital of commercial companies, without specifying the legal regime for the operation.

For its part, the French legislator, through the law of July 24 1966 on commercial companies, considers that the legal regime for the partial contribution of assets is dualist.

Under article 387 of the law of 24-07-1966, the parties may decide to subject the transaction to the demerger regime. In addition to this choice, the parties may also elect to attribute the status of contribution in kind to the partial asset contribution.

The choice of one or other of the two attributions must be justified by the parties according to the purpose of the transaction, since by choosing to treat the partial asset contribution as a so-called partial demerger, the company making the partial contribution consisting of a complete branch of activity, as well as the company receiving the contribution, can benefit from the partial asset contribution being subject to the special merger regime.

By considering the partial contribution of assets as an outright contribution in kind, companies are obliged to apply the ordinary law regime concerning the transfer of the elements incorporated in the contribution.

But whatever the nature of the partial asset contribution, the procedural prerequisites are the same.

In this first part, we will first study the steps involved in setting up a partial contribution of assets. Then, in a second chapter, we will study the tax effects of the partial contribution of assets.

Chapter 1: Stages in the implementation of a partial asset contribution

In practice, the implementation of the partial contribution of assets requires, on the one hand, a preparatory phase (section I) which is characterized by two successive stages, namely the valuation

---

[11] Francis Lefebvre edition: «Pratique des restructurations», page 234.

of the elements of the contribution in question which will be used to calculate the tax base, and the control of this valuation by the competent person. Secondly, the setting up of the partial asset contribution project (section II) is marked by the approval of the project by the competent bodies of the two companies: the contributor and the beneficiary. Once in place, the partial asset contribution project can only take effect once it has been subject to the necessary publicity formalities.

Section I: Stages in the implementation of a partial asset contribution

In general, when a company disposes of an asset, or participates in one or all of its assets, it is not obliged to carry out this operation and dispose of the asset at its historical cost.[12] The value of an asset is not stable; it is subject to fluctuations in the money market on the one hand, and wear and tear which will lead to depreciation of its value on the other.

A partial transfer of assets is the transfer of a set of assets from the transferring company to the receiving company. This transfer can only take place after a valuation of these items, which will serve as the basis for calculating the new value of these assets. Once the new value has been calculated, the partial asset contribution project must be reviewed and approved by the governing bodies of both parties (the transferring company and the beneficiary company), so that the project can be legally implemented.

§1 : Valuation of the Partial Contribution of Assets: a variety of methods

Appraising means assessing the value of a property, and setting a confirmation price between the buyer and seller, both of whom are subject to generally opposing personal motivations.

The purpose of valuing all the assets or the division in which the transferring company participates is to determine the exchange parity.

This parity will determine the number of shares to be issued. This valuation will also enable the exact determination of the rights of the shareholders or associates of the companies concerned.

The valuation also makes it possible to determine whether the transferring company remains responsible for discharging its liabilities, or whether it transfers them to the transferee company.

The valuation relates to all the components of the branch of activity forming the partial asset contribution.

(A) Analysis of industry components :

By definition, an autonomous branch of activity, also known as an autonomous operation, is "all the assets and liabilities of a division of a company which, from an organizational point of view,

---

[12] Historical cost is the value at which an asset was acquired. In accounting terms, the historical value of an asset is the value at which it is recorded on the company's balance sheet.

constitute an autonomous operation, i.e. a unit capable of functioning by its own means"[13] .

In fact, it is the assets and liabilities of the autonomous branch of activity that will be the subject of the valuation in order to be able to determine the overall value of the partial asset contribution at the time of its completion.

Sometimes, in the case of a parent company's subsidiary, an analysis of the subsidiary's income statement forms part of the valuation of the subsidiary involved in the partial asset contribution.

(1) Analysis of asset accounts:

Starting with assets, we need to distinguish between fixed and current assets:

a) Fixed assets :

♦ Intangible assets :

According to universal accounting concepts, intangible assets consist of :

- Research and development costs: this item comprises all expenditure incurred by the production unit on research and new developments covering a number of fields, such as IT, industry, etc., as well as on the development of new products.

- Patents, trademarks and licenses: this balance sheet item includes acquisitions of external patents, as well as trademarks and licenses acquired by the company for its own business.

- Goodwill: historically, goodwill dates back to the 19th[e] century, when it represented the accounting counterpart of contributions in industry remunerated by equity interests or founder's shares. Nowadays, according to the accounting system, goodwill is an excess value.[12] [14] Based on economic studies, we can say that economic indices can be used to roughly estimate the value of goodwill.

♦ Property, plant and equipment :

Starting from an analysis of intangible fixed assets, which seem to be the target of much controversy in terms of valuation, it seems easier to estimate the value of tangible fixed assets, since the starting point is a so-called historical value which may either depreciate over time, as is the case for depreciable fixed assets (buildings, transport equipment, machinery and tools), or appreciate over time for non-depreciable fixed assets (non-depreciable land).

The calculation of the new value of fixed assets is based on various mathematical methods known as depreciation methods.

♦ Long-term investments :

Long-term investments consist of:

- Equity interests, which represent all securities with an operational use and not only those

---

[13] Fiduciary Group RF Dictionary; 2003 edition; page 91.

[14] : In other words, it has no precisely identifiable value.

for which the company has a minimum shareholding in another company.

- Receivables on investments in subsidiaries and affiliates, which are advances made to subsidiaries.

b) Current assets :

The main headings of current assets are :

♦ Inventory accounts include the balances of incoming and outgoing merchandise (in the case of a trading company), raw materials, work-in-progress and finished goods; these accounts can be valued using one of four methods:

     Weighted average unit cost

     The "first in first out" principle

     The "last in last out" principle

     The "last in first out" principle

♦ Customer account: At the level of this account we find the total annual amount of trade receivables in favor of the company but not yet collected.

♦ Cash and cash equivalents: comprise the company's cash and bank balances, or those of the subsidiary involved in the partial asset contribution.

(2) Analysis of liability accounts :

A company's liabilities represent the resources with which it will finance the uses shown on the assets side of its balance sheet.

a) Shareholders' equity :

A company's equity is obtained by subtracting its assets from its total liabilities. It is also known as the company's net worth.

(B) Valuation methods :

For some, it seems obvious that a company's value is measured by its own assets. For others, it can only be assessed on the basis of earnings. Finally, there are valuation methods that combine these two approaches, using the concept of goodwill.

In fact, using either of these methods is not as decisive of the value of the partial contribution if the choice is not justified.

(1) Balance sheet valuation methods :

The industry is valued on the basis of the various balance sheet items, adjusted to obtain their current value. Before explaining the valuation of balance sheet items, it is useful to provide a few definitions:

- Net book value or net position. This value is derived from the company's balance sheet as presented.

<u>Book net assets = Gross assets - Current liabilities</u>

Book value is only very exceptionally used as the basis for a valuation method. It is based on the concept of historical cost, and only includes acquired intangible assets. Free revaluation possibilities only partially correct the difference between historical cost and current value.

- Adjusted net assets or adjusted mathematical value or intrinsic value: this value is based on the book value of net assets, and is determined by giving each balance sheet item its current value, i.e. :

<u>Adjusted net assets = Adjusted gross assets - Adjusted current liabilities</u>

This is the amount of capital that would currently need to be invested to reconstitute the company's used assets in their current state.

Adjusted net assets include only assets required for operating purposes. Unavailable assets are treated separately. Thus, they are recorded at their realizable value net of all costs and taxes, and not at their current value.

- Substantial value: A company is a production tool. This tool is made up of a set of assets of all kinds involved in its operation, regardless of how they are financed.

Substantial value = Total real assets - Non-operating assets + Capital expenditure needed to maintain existing production facilities + Leased assets

The choice of this method also has an influence on the company's results. It corresponds to the real value of the tools that make up the company, i.e. all the assets of all kinds engaged and organized to achieve its purpose. It is not used alone as a valuation method.

- Permanent capital required for operations: This corresponds to the fixed assets required for operations, plus the working capital requirement[15] .

It differs from the substantial value reduced by taking into account the partial working capital requirement, instead of the partial working capital requirement existing at the valuation date.

Like the substantial value, the permanent capital required for operations is only a calculation datum used in valuation methods linked to income. It is therefore necessary to restate this result to make it compatible with the elements used to calculate the permanent capital required for operations.

(2) Profitability-related methods :

Profitability-based methods are based on the following principle: The economic value of an asset is the present value of its future profits.

[14) : Working Capital Requirement (WCR) is the net amount of circulating capital to be permanently immobilized to finance operations. Definition taken from RCF n° 45; 3ieme quarter 1999.

Three methods are generally presented: Yield value; Cash-flow method; Profitability or productivity value.

- Yield value : The yield value of a company is obtained by discounting the dividends distributed over several years, and possibly the residual value of the company.

$$VR = Di /(1+k) + D2/(1+k)^2 +.+Dn/(1+k)^n + Vr/(1+k)^n$$

With :

      PV: company profitability value

      Vr: residual value

      D: expected dividend flow

      k: discount rate

      n: number of years

This valuation method is only suitable for listed companies and those with a rational dividend distribution policy.

- Cash-flow method: In this case, cash-flow corresponds to self-financing capacity. It is equal to the sum of net income, depreciation, amortization and provisions.

$$\text{Enterprise value} = CFi/(1+k) + CF2/(1+k)^2 +.+CFn/(1+k)^n$$

- The profitability value of productivity: This value is obtained by discounting a series of the company's constant profitable capacities.

$$VR= CB/(1+k) +CB/(1+k)^2 +... + CB/(1+k)^n$$

With ;

      PV: Value for money

      CB: earning power

      k: discount rate

      n: number of years

This method is open to criticism because it does not take into account the residual value of the business at period n.

(3) Combined methods :

- The concept of goodwill: Goodwill is the excess of a company's overall value over the sum of the values of its various tangible and intangible assets.

Goodwill is the set of intangible elements that cannot be detached individually, and which contribute to giving the company as a whole a value greater than that of its component parts.

$$VE = ANC + GW$$

With

>EV: enterprise value
>
>ANC: adjusted net assets
>
>GW: goodwill

All these methods have their advantages and disadvantages. When choosing one of them, it is important to be objective, and to select the one that is most profitable for both the transferor and the transferee. In fact, the two companies, by mutual agreement, choose the method best suited to the structure of the branch of activity being transferred and their common interests arising from the adoption of this economic merger.

It should be noted that the valuation stage must be followed by a control of this estimate for fear of exaggerating the value attributed to some of these assets, which may harm the interests of both parties.

In fact, this inspection is carried out by a competent person according to precise procedures.

§2: *Control of the partial asset contribution*

Unlike cash contributions, the value of the assets contributed depends on an estimate that may be deliberately or unintentionally wrong.

When the error stems from an overvaluation, it presents two serious dangers:

Firstly, overestimation unfairly inflates the contribution of the contributor in question and disadvantages his co-partners, particularly those who make a cash contribution.

Secondly, in companies where the company's assets are the only collateral available to creditors, the overvaluation of contributions in kind misleads third parties as to the exact value of the assets used to secure their claims.[16]

For these reasons, it was necessary to take the necessary precautions against the overvaluation of contributions, which can only take place through the appointment of the competent person who is the commissaire aux apports, known in the case of a demerger as the commissaire à la scission.

(A) Appointment of the competent person for the inspection

By analogy with the provisions of the Tunisian Commercial Companies Code, governing demergers and mergers, the appointment of the person responsible for overseeing the partial contribution of

---

[16] AMAMOU Salah; cabinet Amamou; le manuel permanent du droit des affaires tunisien, April 2001

assets is subject to the same rules as for the person responsible for overseeing the merger or demerger.

The person in charge of control is the commissaire aux apports (contributions auditor) if the transaction is treated as a contribution in kind, and a commissaire à la scission (demerger auditor) if it is treated as a demerger.

However, the appointment of the "commissaire aux apport" differs depending on whether it involves the incorporation of a new company or an ordinary capital increase.

(1) When creating a new company

Article 173, paragraph I of the French Commercial Companies Code (Code des Sociétés Commerciales)[17] states that in the event of a contribution in kind, and prior to the incorporation of the company, one or more "commissaires aux apports" (contribution auditors) are appointed by order of the President of the Court of First Instance at the place of the company's registered office, from among legal experts, at the request of the founders.

According to this article, the commissioner is appointed by order of the president of the court of first instance; it is in fact the judge who appoints the commissaire aux apports, whatever the legal form of the company (whether or not it is a public limited company).

In the case of a limited liability company (SARL), in accordance with article 100 CSC paragraph II[18] , the valuation must be carried out by a commissioner appointed unanimously by the partners or, failing this, by an order on request issued by the president of the court of first instance in whose jurisdiction the company's registered office is located.

This order is made at the request of the most diligent future partner.

The principle for SARLs is therefore that the appointment of the statutory auditor is made unanimously by the partners, with the exception that in the event of disagreement, the appointment is made by the courts.

By way of comparison, French legislation requires all joint-stock companies to appoint a commissaire aux apports, regardless of whether the company is incorporated with or without a public offering.

In the case of a new company, how will the statutory auditor be appointed in the event of a capital increase?

(2) At the time of a capital increase

---

[17] Article 173 paragraph 1: "In the event of a contribution in kind and prior to the incorporation of the company, one or more contribution auditors are appointed by order of the President of the Court of First Instance at the location of the company's registered office from among the legal experts, at the request of the founders.

[18] Article 100 paragraph 2: "The valuation of the contribution in kind must be carried out by a contributions auditor, who must be appointed unanimously by the partners, or failing this by an order on request issued by the president of the court of first instance in whose jurisdiction the company's registered office is located. This order is issued at the request of the most diligent future partner.

In the case of a capital increase, the appointment of the commissaire aux apports is made at the request of the Board of Directors or the Management Board, in accordance with article 173 CSC.[19]

Article 135 of the CSC stipulates that: "If the capital increase has been carried out in whole or in part by contributions in kind, the valuation of these contributions will be carried out in accordance with the provisions of article 100 of the present code.

According to this article, the appointment of the statutory auditor for the capital increase is made in the same way as for the incorporation of a company.

It should be noted that, in the case of a SARL (limited liability company), when the value of the assets contributed does not exceed 3,000 dinars, the appointment of a contribution auditor is not mandatory.

However, the introduction of the "commissaire aux apports" is based on a reduction in the liability of partners, which should have repercussions on the liability of the "commissaire".

(B)Authority and responsibility of the person in charge of control

Given the onerous nature of the contribution auditor's responsibilities, the French Code des Sociétés Commerciales has given him a certain amount of power to enable him to carry out his duties.

(1) The powers of the contributions auditor

Power is the ability to act on behalf of someone. In this case, the power of the commissaire aux apports is embodied in his ability to act on behalf of the partners or shareholders in connection with his mission to evaluate the contributions in kind.

This power is accompanied by the commissioner's freedom to choose his or her own working methods and approaches, with the support of his or her team.

In fact, the statutory auditor is only required to draw up a report containing a description of each contribution in kind, its consistency, its method of valuation and its interest for the company.[20]

The Tunisian legislator has not regulated the possibility of assistance in the performance of the commissaire aux apports assignment.

On the other hand, article 64, paragraph 3 of the French decree of 23-03-1967[21] stipulates that the commissaires aux apports may be assisted by one or more experts chosen by them.

Given that this solution makes it possible to make a more reliable judgment on the valuation of the

---

[19] Article 306 CSC: *"In the event of a contribution in kind, one or more contribution auditors are appointed at the request of the Board of Directors or the Management Board in accordance with the provisions of article 173 of the present code.*

[20] Article 173 paragraph 2 CSC: "The auditors are responsible for assessing the value of contributions in kind.

[21] ZARROUK Radhouane: "Le commissariat aux apports: aspects juridiques et techniques de la mission" (Contribution audit: legal and technical aspects of the assignment); dissertation for the end of the public accountancy internship required to obtain the certificate of certified public accountant (expert-comptable inscrit dans l'ordre). 1996 .

contributions; especially in the event of an inability to value certain contributions in kind of a particular type such as: computer software, patent, license...

In other cases, companies can call on a team of "commissaires aux apports" who can work together to ensure maximum fairness between the two companies involved in the transaction.

In order for the statutory auditor to carry out his mission in the most convincing way, he must have the necessary means, documents and information at his disposal.

The statutory auditor may use the report of the company's statutory auditor to verify the existence of certain contributions in kind.

The commissioner can also circularize[22] third parties to obtain information on certain elements.

The Commissioner's broad powers are justified by his heavy responsibilities.

(2) Liability of the contribution auditor

In carrying out his duties, the contributions auditor may incur civil, criminal and even disciplinary liability.

a) Civil liability :

In accordance with article 173 of the Companies Code, the contributions auditor is liable under the conditions of ordinary law for any faults he may have committed in the performance of his duties.

This liability is incurred only if the statutory auditor can be shown to be at fault, and only to the extent of the damage he has caused to the partners, the company and third parties.

These faults can be :

- The overvaluation of contributions, which can be detrimental to the partners or shareholders of the beneficiary company;
- When the contribution auditor submits a report that is insufficient or neglects the necessary information;
- When the contribution auditor takes the liberty of interfering in the company's management, even though he is an independent body.

However, there must be a causal relationship between the fault and the damage caused.

Once this relationship is justified, the contribution auditor also incurs criminal and even disciplinary liability.

b) Criminal liability :

---

[22] YAICH Abdelraouf "Audit and internal control procedures": Circularization, also known as the confirmation procedure, is a method of controlling information concerning the existence of certain assets, which consists in sending to certain third parties, at the request of the auditor, confirmation of the information requested with that provided by the company.

The CSC provides for two criminal offences, namely the offence of illegally exercising the functions of contributions auditor and the offence of fraudulently increasing contributions in kind.

On the one hand, with regard to illegal practice and in accordance with article184 CSC, which stipulates that: "A fine of 1,000 to 10,000 dinars shall be imposed on anyone who has knowingly accepted or retained the duties of contributions auditor contrary to the provisions of article 174 above".

Article 174 of the Companies Code lists the persons who are prohibited from acting as contributions auditor, for reasons of incompatibility.

On the other hand, for the offence of fraudulent mark-up, the legislator has made a distinction between the penalties for a limited liability company and those for a public limited company.

In the case of SARLs, in accordance with article 146 of the CSC, anyone who knowingly and in bad faith causes contributions in kind to be valued at a higher amount than their real value is liable to imprisonment for between one and five years and a fine of between 500 and 5,000 dinars[23] .

In the case of a SA and in application of article 186 CSC, the penalty of imprisonment has remained the same as in the case of a SARL, but the fine has been increased from 1000 to 10000 dinars.[24]

However, in the case of a company not making a public offering, the penalty is limited to a fine[25] .

c) *Disciplinary liability:*

In general, the contribution auditor is a chartered accountant.

This expert is bound by the ethics of the profession to which he belongs. Should he commit a fault, he will be liable to disciplinary sanctions.

These sanctions vary according to the degree of error committed, and the expert may be reprimanded or even prohibited from practicing his profession.

If the commissioner is a legal expert, he may be struck off the list of legal experts.

d) *Tax liability:*

In addition to criminal, civil and disciplinary liability, the commissaire aux apports is also a statutory auditor. By virtue of this qualification, he is liable for tax purposes.

Indeed, under article 99 paragraph I of section III of chapter II «Penal tax penalties» of the (Tunisian) code of tax rights and procedures, the contributions auditor may be subject to tax penalties in the

---

[23] Article 164 CSC: *"Shall be punished by imprisonment of one to 5 years and a fine of 500 to 5,000 dinars. [...] 2- persons who knowingly and in bad faith, cause contributions in kind to be valued higher than their real value".*
[24] Article 186 CSC: *"Those who, by means of fraudulent maneuvers, attribute to their contribution in kind a valuation higher than its real value are liable to a prison sentence of one to five years and a fine of 1,000 to 10,000 dinars [...] 4.* When the company does not make a public offering, the penalty is limited to a fine.
[25] Article cited above.

event of misconduct deemed to be intentional and wilful[26] .

However, it is difficult to assess the intentional element of this fault, as up to now the legislator has not dealt with cases of litigation involving the liability of the commissaire aux apports. Indeed, the latter carries out his mission while respecting his independence.

This is essentially justified by the heavy civil, criminal and, above all, disciplinary penalties involved.

Section II: Setting up the project

In this case, the contribution auditor's opinion will be expressed in the form of a valuation report on the branch of activity contributed.

The purpose of this report is to inform shareholders or associates about the nature of the elements contained in the contribution and the valuation method adopted, as well as the reasons why this method was chosen.

In his report, the statutory auditor must also state that the value of the contributions corresponds at least to the amount of the capital they represent, plus any additional paid-in capital.

If the partial contribution of assets is subject to the demerger regime, the so-called demerger commissioner is required to prepare a written report on the terms of the partial contribution of assets, verifying that the relative value assigned to the companies' shares is appropriate and that the exchange ratio is fair.

In this way, the statutory auditor must check the partial asset contribution project already drawn up by the two companies involved in the transaction.

The contribution auditor's control is just one of the steps required to complete the partial asset contribution project.

This report, together with the draft partial asset contribution agreement, must be submitted to the relevant decision-making bodies for approval.

§1: Bodies empowered to make adoption decisions

Whether considered as a contribution in kind or subject to the demerger regime, the proposed

---

[26] Article 99 paragraph I: *"Business agents, tax consultants, experts and any other persons who are self-employed in keeping or assisting in the keeping of accounts and who have knowingly drawn up or helped to draw up false accounts or false accounting documents with the aim of undermining the tax base or the tax itself, shall be liable to imprisonment for a term of sixteen days to three years and a fine of 1,000 dinars to 50,000 dinars, in addition to the withdrawal of their licence to practise. Such persons shall also be jointly and severally liable with their clients for payment of the principal amount of the tax and related penalties evaded by their actions. Such persons are also jointly and severally liable with their clients for payment of the principal tax and related penalties evaded by their actions.*

partial asset contribution must be submitted for approval before it can be legally implemented.

This approval is different when the partial asset contribution is considered as a contribution in kind or a demerger.

(A) If the partial contribution is considered as a contribution in kind

On the contributing company's side, the transaction constitutes an act of management in that there will be no correlative revision of the contributing company's bylaws, i.e. no capital reduction resulting from the partial contribution.

Under Tunisian law, since the partial contribution of assets is a priori a form of ordinary capital increase, it is a management transaction as long as the parties have not opted to make it subject to the preferential merger regime.

By way of comparison, the French law of July 24, 1966 is clear on this issue, and specifically in article 226 announces that sometimes the partial contribution of assets is considered as a management transaction if it has not been placed under the legal regime of company mergers or demergers.

Under Tunisian law, the adoption of the partial contribution agreement is the responsibility of the Chairman of the Board of Directors, the Management Board or even the Managing Director when the contributing company is not a public limited company.

Under French law, the partial contribution of assets, which is not subject to the demerger regime, does not require the approval of shareholders or associates, the convening of special meetings of shareholders or holders of investment certificates, or the convening of an extraordinary meeting of bondholders[27] .

On the part of the company receiving the partial asset contribution, the transaction is analyzed as a company formation by contribution in kind if the beneficiary is a new company.

If the beneficiary company already exists, the capital will be increased by a special type of contribution in kind.

According to the Tunisian Commercial Code, in the case of a capital increase, the partial contribution of assets must be approved by the general meeting of shareholders or associates ruling under the majority and quorum conditions required to amend the bylaws.

---

[27]   Edition juris-classeur société 1998; fascicule 164-10 page 6

(B) The partial contribution is treated as a demerger

According to article 429 of the Commercial Companies Code[28] , the draft of the partial contribution of assets subject to the demerger regime must be made available to shareholders two months before the Extraordinary General Meeting called to approve the contributions in kind contained in the branch of activity, in accordance with the conditions required by the Code and specific to each form of company.

For its part, the French legislator considers that the partial contribution of assets governed by the demerger regime must, on pain of nullity, be adopted by the shareholders under the conditions of quorum and majority laid down by the law of July 24, 1966 relating to commercial companies, or by the extraordinary general meeting of shareholders.

Approval of the demerger can only be given after examination of the reports of the Board of Directors or the demerger auditor.

In addition, when the partial contribution is made to a pre-existing company, the shareholders must decide on :

- Approval of the proposed partial asset contribution, capital increase and amendment to the bylaws.
- Valuation of contributions in kind.

When the partial asset contribution is made to a new company, the approval is made according to the rules specific to the corporate form chosen for the said company.

If the company is a limited liability partnership, it is the partners who will act as founders of the new company.

If the new company is a public limited company (SA), the draft articles of association are approved by the extraordinary general meeting of the transferring company, while for the receiving company, approval is given by the constituent general meeting.

In the event of the existence of bondholders in the transferring company, the draft partial asset contribution is submitted to the bondholders' meetings upon a simple request made by them, without the need to consult the said meeting.

§2: Date and effect of decision

For the partial contribution of assets to take effect, the draft report drawn up by the contributions auditor must be submitted to the competent bodies of both companies. This report must then be approved, and the necessary publicity formalities carried out.

---

[28] Article 429 of the CSC: "*A demerger can only be carried out after a merger plan has been drawn up and submitted to the Extraordinary General Meeting for approval under the same conditions as the merger..*".

(A) Project approval :

Any such approval will only take effect from the date on which the Extraordinary General Meetings of the companies required to complete the transaction are held.

In fact, the said project must have been approved by the general meeting of the transferring company, and it must have been declared that the autonomous branch of activity that was the subject of the contribution was automatically detached from the parent company on the day of the final completion of the partial asset contribution transaction.

In addition, the shareholders or associates of the beneficiary company must have given their final approval at an Extraordinary General Meeting to the contributions resulting from the proposed partial asset contribution, and must have carried out the resulting capital increases.

But the object of the partial asset contribution project must meet the mandatory conditions of the July 29, 1991 law on competition and pricing.

On the one hand, for the beneficiary company, the adoption of the proposed partial asset contribution must not prevent, restrict or distort competition in the market.

In accordance with article 5[29] of the law of July 29, 1991 modified by the law of April 24, 1995.

The project is prohibited when it will restrict market access to other companies or the free exercise of competition, or even share markets or sources of supply.

Acceptance of the proposed partial asset contribution is given by the Competition Council in accordance with the provisions of the aforementioned law.

In addition, and in accordance with article 7 of the said law[30] , any merger project or operation likely to create a dominant position on the domestic market or a substantial part of this market, must be submitted to the Ministry of Commerce for approval.

In addition, the Competition Council, when ruling on the proposed partial asset contribution, may require the Ministry's agreement to the project before it is published.

(B) Project publicity :

In accordance with article 16 of the French Commercial Code, partial asset contributions are subject to filing and publication formalities.

---

[29] Article5: *"Concerted actions and express or tacit agreements aimed at preventing, restricting or distorting competition on the market are prohibited when they tend to :*
2/limit market access to other companies or the free exercise of competition.
4/ share markets or sources of supply".
[30] Article? *Any merger project or operation likely to create a dominant position on the domestic market or a substantial part of this market must be submitted to the Ministry of Commerce for approval.*

According to article 432 of the CSC[31] , the draft demerger (in this case, a partial contribution of assets) voted by the Extraordinary General Meeting must be published in the Official Gazette of the Republic of Tunisia, and in two daily newspapers, one of which is in Arabic, within one month of the date of the last meeting.

For its part, the French legislator distinguishes between the effective date of the partial asset transaction, depending on whether it is assessed with regard to third parties or with regard to the participating companies.

Article 374, paragraph 3 of the French law of July 24, 1966[32] stipulates that a declaration of conformity of the project must be drawn up and filed with the clerk of the commercial court, failing which the partial contribution of assets subject to the demerger regime will be null and void. This declaration must be made by the companies involved in the transaction, and signed by at least one director, a member of the management board or the manager of each of the companies having received a mandate for this purpose.

With regard to third parties, the partial contribution of assets only becomes enforceable once the necessary amending entries have been made in the Trade and Companies Register.

Between participating companies, the effective date of a partial contribution differs depending on whether it is made to a new or an existing company.

In the case of a new company, the partial asset contribution takes effect on the date of registration of the beneficiary company in the Commercial Register.

In this case, the effective date is the date of the last General Meeting approving the transaction.

Chapter 2: Tax effects of the partial contribution of assets

The partial contribution of assets is a transaction whereby a company, known as the contributor, contributes an element or part of its assets, or an autonomous operating unit, to the capital of another company, known as the beneficiary of this contribution, in exchange for shares. The special nature of this contribution has given rise to debate about its tax implications. Faced with this debate, the Tunisian legislator, as in procedural matters, remains silent on the tax treatment of this operation. For the Tunisian legislator, the partial contribution of assets is a simple form of capital increase. However, if we refer to Tunisian doctrine and the internal documentation of the Tunisian tax authorities, we find that both adopt the term "corporate restructuring operation". This adoption has its origins in French and EU legislation, and we have simply borrowed the term.

The adoption of this restructuring operation, or according to the Tunisian legislator, capital increase

---

[31] Article432 CSC: "*The demerger decision taken by the Extraordinary General Meeting must be published in the Journal Officiel de la République Tunisienne and in two daily newspapers, one of which is in Arabic.*
[32] See appendix 3 (chapter on mergers and demergers in the law of 24-07-1966 on commercial companies).

operation, is explained for companies.

The transfer of the elements of the partial asset contribution has tax implications in terms of both direct and indirect taxation.

According to OUDENOT Philippe: "A partial contribution of assets constituting a transfer of assets and liabilities from one company to another entails in principle, with regard to registration duties, the payment of transfer duties and, with regard to corporate income tax, the consequences of a partial cessation of business, in particular the immediate taxation of capital gains and provisions relating to the elements contributed[33] ".

The transfer of a partial contribution has both direct and indirect tax implications. However, the parties may submit the transaction to the general tax regime, in which case the scope of this regime will concern both direct and indirect taxes.

Admittedly, the parties voluntarily choose to submit the partial asset contribution transaction to the common law tax regime, but this choice is not arbitrary, as it is in the common interest of both parties.

Section I: Scope of the general tax system :

It is left to the prerogative of the transferor and transferee companies to decide whether or not to subject the partial asset contribution transaction to the ordinary law regime.

From an accounting point of view, this transaction is analyzed as an exceptional sale for the contributing company. The transferee company, on the other hand, records a capital increase.

The submission of a partial contribution to the common system of tax law entails taxation of the result of the valuation of the contribution. This section examines the scope of this system, firstly in terms of direct taxation (§1) and then in terms of indirect taxation (§2).

§1: Direct taxes

The valuation of the partial asset contribution served as the basis for determining the taxable amount. The taxable amount thus calculated shows either a capital gain or a capital loss. A capital gain arises when a fixed asset is sold at a price higher than its book value, or its acquisition cost in the case of a non-depreciable asset. Book value is defined as the acquisition value of the asset less depreciation. A capital loss occurs when, on the other hand, the actual value of the item sold falls below its book value.

Hence the meaning of the term "capital gain" or "capital loss" can only be fiscal, since any capital gain realized on the disposal of fixed assets is taxable, whereas the capital loss is deductible.

---

[33] OUDENOT Philippe: Fiscalité approfondie des sociétés, Paris 2001, page 695.

A partial contribution may include fixed assets whose appraised value differs from their historical cost, resulting in a capital gain (A). In addition to fixed assets, the partial contribution is by definition linked to the notion of branch of activity, which in turn encompasses other elements that are subject to other taxes (B).

(A) Real estate capital gains :

When a company disposes of an asset forming part of its fixed assets (furniture, leasehold rights, machinery and equipment, etc.), it generally makes a profit, insofar as the purchase price is less than the fair market value.

is higher than the book value of the asset sold. According to the balance sheet theory applied by the French income and corporation tax codes, this capital gain is included in taxable profit. This profit is distinguished by its occasional nature.

In this case, the partial asset contribution is a contribution like any other type of company contribution, with the contributing company receiving equity securities in return for its contribution. However, legal experts consider the partial asset contribution to be a special type of contribution in kind, or even a partial disposal of the contributing company. Considering the partial contribution as a partial disposal means that it is subject to the capital gains regime.

The partial contribution of assets comprises assets and liabilities, the assets of the contribution are composed of depreciable and non-depreciable fixed assets, the treatment and calculation of the capital gain relating to these fixed assets.

(1) In the case of non-depreciable fixed assets :

There are both depreciable and non-depreciable fixed assets on a company's balance sheet. However, the fact that these items are non-depreciable does not prevent them from being valued. The estimated value of these assets may give rise to capital gains or losses.

The tax treatment of this income is well defined by the Tunisian corporate income tax code.

A capital gain or loss is the difference between the price of an asset on the balance sheet, i.e. its historical cost, and its current value, i.e. the value resulting from a revaluation of the asset.

Under the Tunisian tax code, capital gains arising on the transfer of an asset from one company to another are taxable in the hands of the transferring company.[34] In this case, the partial contribution of assets is considered to be a pure and simple contribution, which means that it may only include non-depreciable items such as goodwill, whose value is by nature constantly increasing, except in very rare cases. Subsequently, under Tunisian tax legislation, the transferring company is required to include the resulting capital gain in its annual profit as exceptional income.

---

[34] AYADI Habib: Droit fiscal; impôt sur les revenus des personnes physiques et impôt sur les sociétés, Tunis, CERP, 1996.

The Tunisian IS code places this capital gain on non-depreciable real estate in the company's property income category, as part of the company's occasional activities.

(2) In the case of depreciable fixed assets :

For depreciable fixed assets such as buildings, machinery and equipment ... . If the company makes a contribution in this category, it is necessary to assess the current value of the asset, since this differs from the historical value entered on the balance sheet. Calculating this new value reveals either a capital gain or a capital loss. In order to determine the capital gain or loss, the amount of special costs relating to the sale and the amount of accumulated depreciation up to the date of sale must be deducted from the sale price. The result is a capital gain if it exceeds the sale price, and a capital loss if it does not.

The income tax and corporate income tax codes provide for the reintegration of capital gains into the profit and loss account of the transferring company, under the same conditions as for non-depreciable fixed assets.

In the case of a capital gain (which really makes the difference between depreciable and non-depreciable fixed assets), this is deductible from the transferring company's income.

In this case, the Tunisian legislator considers a partial contribution to be a contribution in kind, which generates a capital gain, to be subject to the same conditions as the transfer of ordinary assets.

The transferring company considers the partial transfer of assets to the receiving company as a sale of all its assets. It will be required to include the capital gain in determining its taxable profit for the year in which the transaction is carried out. Although this exceptional income will not be distributed to the company's shareholders, it must be taxed in accordance with current tax legislation. In fact, the company benefiting from the capital gain is required to file a capital gains tax return when the transaction is actually carried out, and at the latest by the end of the third month following that in which the sale is actually carried out[35] .

Under Tunisian tax legislation, a partial contribution of assets considered as a contribution in kind is a partial disposal of the assets of the contributing company, which triggers the taxation of this so-called exceptional profit.

We will try to illustrate an example of calculating the capital gain on the sale of a depreciable asset under Tunisian tax law:

On 01-01-2002, a company sold equipment and tools at a price of 12,000DT. The acquisition price was 18000DT (the acquisition date is 01-01-1997).

Depreciation from date of acquisition to date of sale at 10% = 18000*10%*5 = 9000 DT

---

[35] AYADI Habib: Droit fiscal; impôt sur les revenus des personnes physiques et impôt sur les sociétés, Tunis, CERP, 1996.

The book value of the equipment = 18000-9000 = 9000 DT

The capital gain on the sale is taxable or, in the case of a partial contribution, can be added back in the calculation of the company's income = 12000-9000 = 3000 DT

Conclusion: this capital gain generated by a partial contribution of assets and which must be added back to income for 2002 is 3,000 DT.

Example of calculating the capital gain on the contribution of a non-depreciable asset :

On 01-01-2002, a company transfers a business or license to another company for a value of 20,000 TD. This asset was acquired by the transferor on 01-01-1998 at 7000 DT.

Capital gain = 20000-7000 = 13000 DT

Conclusion: The capital gain generated by this contribution and to be reintegrated into the profit and loss account of the transferring company is 13,000 DT.

The Tunisian legislator thus considers the partial contribution to be subject to the ordinary tax regime as an ordinary transfer. French law recognizes the adoption of the ordinary tax regime for partial asset contributions as a general principle, with one exception: the possibility of placing this operation under the special regime known as the "régime de faveur des fusions". In fact, the common law regime under French law is known as the *régime des cessions* or *régime de cessation partielle d'activité.*

(B) Tax aspects of other components of the contribution :

Some authors define a partial asset contribution as a branch of activity capable of operating on its own. Throughout its life, this production unit has made profits and losses. What will be the tax treatment of the resulting loss?

In addition, the transferring company may choose not to retain the equity securities acquired as consideration for the contribution. In this case, how will the distribution be treated?

In the absence of legal rules governing the transfer of these elements of the contribution, Tunisian jurists have tried to find a solution: to consider the partial contribution as a partial transfer, which means that no clear and specific approach can be found for each of the aforementioned elements. To fill this gap in Tunisian law, it has been necessary to refer to both French and European law to answer the questions raised above.

(1) Taxation of worldwide profits in cross-border transactions :

Under Tunisian tax law, the question of transferring losses in the context of a partial asset contribution subject to ordinary tax law remains unanswered. For this reason, it was necessary to review both French and European tax law.

On the one hand, the transferee company is obliged to pay tax on profits not yet taxed at the time of the partial transfer of assets (where the profit or loss of the branch of activity is determined separately from the company to which the branch of activity to which the transfer relates belonged). If, on the other hand, there are provisions relating to the branch of business contributed that have not yet been reintegrated, these must be taxed in the hands of the contributing company.

However, when referring to French law, we must also consider Community law. Directive 90/434/EEC of *July 23, 1990* on the common system of taxation applicable to mergers, divisions, partial transfers of assets and exchanges of shares largely settles the difficulties associated with cross-border corporate restructuring operations.

In fact, these operations, and in particular the partial contribution of assets, are subject to tax legislation that is as different as it is competing. The directive takes as its starting point the various disparities that exist, but does not envisage a harmonization of legislation, but provides for a Community regime to be applied in each Member State to one of these operations. This directive is in addition to existing domestic regimes, which continue to apply while adapting to the new tax regime. The new system is designed not only to avoid taxation in the event of a partial transfer, but also to safeguard the financial interests of both the transferring and the receiving company.

Concerning partial transfers of assets between companies in different Member States, or so-called cross-border transactions.

Pursuant to Article 10, paragraph 2 of Title IV of the Directive, if the transferring company in a Member State applies the worldwide profit tax system (worldwide profit is determined by derogation from the principle of territoriality, and French companies may, with approval, be allowed to determine their taxable profits by taking into account all their French profits and the profits of their direct foreign operations: For example, if a French company has a worldwide taxable profit ([36]), that State may tax the capital gains of the permanent establishment (a permanent establishment may be defined as "a body dependent on an enterprise whose center of management is situated abroad, and which nevertheless has sufficient autonomy for a fraction of the results of the said enterprise to be attributable to it economically and fiscally"), Article 5 of the OECD Model Convention defines a permanent establishment as "the fixed place of business through which an enterprise carries on all or part of its activities") resulting from the adoption of the partial asset contribution transaction, provided that this State allows the deduction of this capital gain in the State where the permanent establishment of the transferring company is located. The State must also allow the deduction of this capital gain in the same way if it was actually established and paid for[37].

---

[36] Dictionnaire RF Groupe Fiduciaire, Fiscal 2003; page 137.

[37] Article 10 paragraph 2, title IV of the directive of 23-07-1990: "...where the Member State of the transferring company applies a system of taxation of worldwide profits, that State shall have the right to tax the profits or capital gains of the permanent establishment arising from the merger, division or transfer of assets, provided that it allows the

(2) The fate of deficits :

Prior to the partial transfer of assets, the branch of activity may be loss-making. In accounting terms, the deficit appears on the liabilities side of the branch's balance sheet. If the beneficiary company does not plan to change its business, the transferring company's losses relating to the transfer can be carried forward to offset future taxable income[38] .

In addition to deferring the tax loss, the partial transfer of assets also makes deferred depreciation commonplace[39] (deferred depreciation is depreciation actually booked during a year with a tax loss, and which the company decides to isolate from the ordinary tax loss in order to be able to carry forward for an unlimited period to subsequent years[40]). As a result of the adoption of the ordinary law regime, the transferring company will no longer be entitled to carry forward deferred amortization against its annual loss.

§2: Indirect taxes

The transfer of partial contribution items also has indirect tax implications. In fact, given the branch of activity group of items necessary to the business such as inventories, receivables....

In terms of indirect taxes, we'll be looking at the impact on VAT as well as registration and stamp duties.

(A) VAT :

Under the terms of Article 9 of the VAT Code, in the event of the sale, contribution to a company, change of use of these assets and in the event of the cessation or abandonment of taxable status, a repayment must be made equal to the amount of value-added tax deducted or which should have been paid, or which has been reimbursed, reduced by 1/5 per calendar year or fraction of a calendar year of ownership in the case of buildings[41] .

The amount of tax subject to adjustment must be stated on the sales invoice or contribution document, regardless of the value of the asset or contribution.

As far as VAT is concerned, Tunisian law is clearer. In fact, in the case of an economic concentration operation such as a merger, demerger, partial contribution of assets or a change in the legal form of a company, the tax or the balance of the value-added tax paid on goods and values qualifying for deduction is transferred to the new company[42] . In this case, the residual tax will be transferred from the transferring company to the transferee company.

---

deduction of the tax which, in the absence of the provisions of this Directive, would have been charged on such profits or capital gains in the State in which the permanent establishment is situated, and that it allows such deduction in the amount which it would have done if the tax had actually been assessed and paid. "

[38] OUDENOT Philippe: Fiscalité approfondie des sociétés, Paris, Litec, 2001, page 725.

[39] Dictionnaire du Groupe Fiduciaire, Fiscal 2003; page 90.

[40] Dictionnaire du Groupe Fiduciaire, Fiscal 2003; page 66.

[41] REZGUI Salah: Code de la TVA et du droit de Consommation commenté et mis à jour, Tunis, PIORT,2001.

[42] Ditto

In fact, if the branch of activity transferred is subject to VAT on an autonomous basis, a declaration of cessation of activity must be filed with the tax authorities within one month of the transaction, together with payment of the relevant duties[43] .

The French legislator, for his part, requires the declaration to be made in order to transfer the VAT credit relating to the branch of activity.

(B) Registration and stamp duties :

When all the elements making up the partial contribution are transferred, the fixed assets, whether tangible or intangible, must be registered with the land registry.

However, the transfer of these assets may be either in ownership or in use, so the treatment will differ.

In terms of registration and stamp duty, the partial asset contribution operation, like any restructuring operation leading to the formation of a new company, or the increase in the share capital of the beneficiary company, must be marked by the completion of the deed that gives rise to the following duties:

- Outright contribution rights ;
- Capital duty ;
- Subscription and payment rights.

The partial contribution of assets is considered to be a special type of contribution in kind. In this respect, the transaction is treated as a partial transfer of the assets of the transferring company. This transfer obliges the beneficiary company to pay the registration and stamp duties corresponding to the acquisition of these assets.

The Tunisian legislator has treated the transaction as a transfer of a set of assets, for which only the beneficiary company will be liable.

The transfer of ownership is considered as a transfer of fixed assets, which must be registered in accordance with certain conditions, depending on the nature of the asset transferred. All transfers must be accompanied by a private deed subject to a fixed registration fee.

In addition, in accordance with Article 23 of the Registration and Stamp Code, the beneficiary company must pay a fixed duty of 100 dinars on the capital increase deed and 5 dinars on any document accompanying the contribution deed.

The legislator seems to have created a preferential regime within the ordinary law system. Indeed, given that the partial contribution is, on the one hand, a transfer of certain assets for the transferring company and, on the other hand, a capital increase or incorporation of a new company for the recipient company, this seems logical given the logic of the transaction. However, in both cases,

---

[43] AMAMOU Salah: Le manuel permanent du droit fiscal et du droit de douane Tunisien, Tunis, Amamou, 1997.

only the receiving company will have to pay the registration duties on the fixed assets, resulting in double taxation for the receiving company. Does the legislator not allow a choice between the two cases? This does not appear to be provided for in the Registration and Stamp Code, and is unlikely to give rise to any disputes, given the absence of any court rulings on the subject.

In the case of a transfer of fixed assets in jouissance and by application of article 31 of the said code, the registration duty due in the case of a transfer in jouissance is liquidated on the price expressed in the lease contract increased by the charges imposed on the beneficiary company[44]. It should be noted that registration duty cannot be levied on a sum greater than the annual lease price plus the charges imposed on the beneficiary company.

Section II: The advantages of adopting the common law system :

The creation of a common tax law regime for partial asset contributions is justified by the interest that this regime represents for both the transferring and the receiving company.

However, the rationale behind the choice of this restructuring operation is not identical for all companies, as each has its own management strategy. The adoption of the common law regime varies according to the intention of the transferring company to retain its equity interests, and of the receiving company to continue in the same business sector: this is the short-term strategy of both the transferring and the receiving companies.

§1: At the level of the transferring company

The common law regime is appropriate for the transferring company insofar as it does not intend to keep the shares returned to it through the partial asset contribution transaction. In other words, the transferring company intends to sell the shares in the short term.

This situation is conceivable in cases where the transferring company, through this economic restructuring operation, has a speculative policy: the company wishes to obtain "the best price" for its contribution[45]. The adoption of the ordinary law regime by the transferring company in this case relieves it of any taxation of the capital gain generated by the partial asset contribution.

In addition to the desire to avoid its tax obligations, the transferring company may choose to adopt the ordinary law system for the following reason:

When the transferring company has incurred losses which, in its opinion, can be carried forward for one of the following reasons: the shortness of the loss carry-forward period, or a change in the company's field of activity. In this case, the transferring company should opt for the standard

---

[44] BESBES Slim: Code annoté des droits d'enregistrement et de timbre, Sfax, 2000, page 61.

[45] Joly sociétés: tax treatment of mergers, demergers and partial contributions of assets; June 2001.

corporate tax regime. In this case, the company will generate taxable capital gains, but these will be offset against its losses.

However, the beneficiary company may also choose to take advantage of the opportunity to make the partial asset contribution it has just adopted subject to the ordinary law regime.

§2: At the beneficiary company level :

For the company benefiting from the partial contribution of assets, this choice will allow it to be relieved of any tax obligation relating to the reintegration of capital gains on the contribution, which is the counterpart of the exemption enjoyed by the contributing company[46].

In addition to the standard capital gains regime for partial asset contributions, the French legislator has also introduced a standard distribution tax regime.

For this category of tax, we have to look at the transferring company, which will receive the equity securities in return for its partial contribution of assets to the receiving company.

In general, when a company distributes securities held in its portfolio among its shareholders, this transaction will be considered for corporate income tax purposes as a dividend distribution, generating real estate income that will be taxable in the hands of each recipient of this income.

Pursuant to Article 112 of the French General Tax Code, this income will not be taxable if the distribution is a repayment of contributions or sums treated as contributions.

However, the common law regimes in Tunisia and France have addressed the issue of registration duties on fixed assets transferred through a partial contribution of assets.

Joly sociétés: tax treatment of mergers, demergers and partial contributions of assets; June 2001

Part Two: The original tax treatment of partial asset contributions

The modern demands of the economic environment have led companies to adopt various restructuring methods, such as demergers, mergers and partial asset contributions.

The merger may be justified by a desire to combat increasingly fierce competition under the best possible conditions.

The partial contribution of assets, on the other hand, has a contrasting justification. On the one hand, it can be a means of combating competition. On the other hand, the partial contribution is itself a technique of inter-firm competition, through the takeover of one firm by another competitor.

However, restructuring enables companies to strengthen their response capabilities and become less vulnerable to ongoing changes in their environment. If the company's objectives are to consolidate its local reputation, increase its market share, or embark on ambitious, less costly projects, then restructuring operations appear to be an appropriate procedure.

Of course, a partial contribution of assets is the most important way of increasing the capital of the beneficiary company.

Indeed, given the legal vacuum and the virtual absence of tax texts dealing with the partial contribution of assets, it is considered in the majority of cases as having a dual system. The legislative authorities leave the choice of the appropriate regime to the will of the parties.

It is up to the two parties to decide whether or not to apply the preferential merger regime to the partial contribution of assets. But this choice is linked to the verification of certain conditions. By definition, a partial contribution of assets means that the contributing company contributes part of its assets and liabilities, or an autonomous branch of activity, to the beneficiary company, with the aim of acquiring a stake in the latter's share capital. This definition underlines the presence of the notion of liabilities as well as that of an autonomous branch of activity.

A merger is a transaction in which the transferring or absorbed company transfers all its assets and liabilities to a receiving or absorbing company, in return for a certain amount of money as consideration for its contribution. This amount is then distributed to the shareholders, as the transferring company disappears following the transaction.

The partial contribution of assets and the merger both have characteristics in common, or at least the partial contribution of assets borrows some criteria from the merger, which justifies the possibility of implicitly placing the partial contribution under the merger regime (chapter I).

Unfortunately, the Tunisian legislator was not explicit about the tax treatment of the contribution. According to the literature, partial asset contributions in Tunisia are subject to the special merger regime. Moreover, the Tunisian tax authorities use almost the same procedures for the adoption of the partial contribution operation as for the merger and demerger. The almost automatic referral of partial contributions to mergers is explained by the simplicity of the projects adopted, the absence of giant companies with a monopoly in the economy, and the rarity of cross-border operations.

Hence the partial contribution of assets can be classed as one of the least complex restructuring operations, which explains the economic and even tax advantages of adopting the preferential merger regime (chapter II).

Chapter 1: The possibility of implicitly placing the partial asset contribution under the merger regime

In a partial asset contribution transaction, a company may contribute only part of its assets to another existing or specially created company, while retaining the remainder.

In this respect, the term "partial" is related to the notion of asset, which must be perceived as a patrimony, i.e. "a contribution in kind that may be encumbered by a liability"""""".

Other definitions consider a partial contribution to be the contribution of a production unit capable by its own means of operating autonomously. As mentioned in the introduction, this unit comprises assets and liabilities. This production unit can be likened to a subsidiary of a parent company, which is none other than the transferring company.

By analogy, a merger is the operation whereby an absorbed company contributes all its assets and liabilities to an absorbing company, in order to increase the capital of the absorbing company or create a new company.

By comparing the two definitions, merger and partial asset contribution have points in common, such as the objective of the operation and the notion of contribution. On the other hand, the consequence of the merger is the disappearance of the transferring company, whereas the partial contribution of assets enables the transferring company to retain the remainder of its assets, thereby preserving its legal personality.

In addition to mergers and partial contributions of assets, demergers are operations whereby a company splits up and transfers all its assets and liabilities to one or more other companies, without being dissolved.

By comparing the two concepts of demerger and partial contribution, we highlight the criterion of preserving the company's legal personality.

On the basis of this comparison, would it be legitimate to consider a partial asset contribution as a demerger? A demerger involves the break-up of all the company's assets and liabilities, whereas a partial contribution affects only part of the company: the partial contribution of assets is a partial demerger. The first section of this chapter analyzes the optional nature of the preferential regime. In the second section, we look at the preferential treatment of mergers.

<u>Section I: The optional nature of submission :</u>

Under different legal systems, whether Tunisian or French, the partial contribution of assets is destined to have a dual system. Depending on the choice of the two parties and the composition of the contribution, the partial asset contribution will either be subject to the ordinary law regime, or to the special merger regime.

However, the fact that the partial contribution is subject to the merger regime does not entail any changes throughout the procedure for its adoption, which remains the same for all restructuring operations, or even all capital increase operations. However, the tax treatment is subject to adoption of the tax rules governing mergers. This adoption is optional, non-mandatory and non-automatic. Certain conditions must be met if the partial contribution is to be legitimately subject to the merger tax regime.

In this section, we will study the notion of autonomous branch of activity (§1), which is the primary condition for benefiting from this special regime. We will then analyse other conditions of comparable importance (§2).

§1 : The concept of an autonomous branch of activity

An autonomous or complete branch of activity is: "the whole of the elements invested in a division of company which constitutes, from the technical point of view, an autonomous exploitation, i.e. a unit able to function by its own means[47] ".

Unfortunately, the Tunisian legislator has not had the merit of defining or outlining the notion of branch of activity, despite the fact that it is one of the most widely used modalities in the Tunisian business world. Admittedly, the majority of Tunisian firms fall into the category of small and medium-sized enterprises. However, our entrepreneurs tend to prefer the adoption of this operation, especially in the case of companies in difficulty. Managers opt for a partial rescue by selling the branch or subsidiary that presents the most danger to the company, and by participating with another company that seems financially more capable of managing this production unit. In this way, the partial asset contribution has its advantages.

In order to define this concept, we had to refer to the definition put forward by French doctrine or adopted by European Community directive no. 90/434 of July 23, 1990.

An autonomous or self-sufficient branch of activity is a combination of assets and liabilities. The composition of the branch of activity is what makes the partial contribution of assets original, and distinguishes it from other types of contributions.

Indeed, by analyzing the characteristics of the branch of activity (A), we will be able to extract the similarities that exist between the partial contribution of assets represented by the contribution of the branch of activity and the other methods of restructuring companies (B).

---

[47] CASIMIR J-Pierre and CHADEFAUX Marital: Partial contribution of assets and complete branch of activity.

(A) Characteristics of the autonomous branch :

The contribution of a complete branch of activity consists of all the assets and liabilities invested in a company division which, from a technical point of view, constitutes an autonomous operation, i.e. a unit capable of functioning by its own means under normal conditions[48].

This definition underlines the presence of two essential characteristics: the autonomous and complete nature of the branch, and the presence of liabilities and assets.

An autonomous and complete branch: autonomy is the ability of an organization to make decisions in relation to a central authority or hierarchy[49]. In this case, the autonomy of the branch of activity to which the contribution relates implies that the activity is actually carried out and assessed by the meetings held. In fact, the French authorities are content to indicate what they do not consider to be a real exercise of the business, without defining the notion of real exercise of the business.

For this branch to be complete, the transfer must relate to all the branch's assets and liabilities, i.e. all the elements associated with the production unit must be transferred. To be productive, the branch of activity must present the optimum combination of assets and liabilities, hence the transfer must relate to all assets and liabilities.

What's more, to be productive, equipment must be operated by people. In fact, the complete and autonomous nature of the branch requires the presence of its own personnel. There must be a transfer of the employment contracts corresponding to these personnel. "The French administration has adopted the postulate that there can be no autonomy without the human resources that drive the[50] activity. Legally, this assumption can be countered. In fact, the transferring company is not obliged to transfer the employment contracts of the staff involved in this branch; it can simply conclude service contracts and keep its staff.

In addition to the transfer of these two elements, the autonomy of the branch of activity is marked by two other criteria of autonomy, one called internal, the other external.

Concerning internal autonomy: the branch of activity is said to be autonomous from the company to which it belongs. The very composition of the branch must demonstrate its independence from all production units. In this respect, the branch of activity must include elements deemed necessary for the operation, thus guaranteeing a long-term supply.

As for external autonomy: this corresponds to the operation of the branch, with regard to the corresponding sector of activity. This criterion seems more economic than fiscal. Indeed, the external autonomy of the branch of activity is analyzed in relation to the organization of the

---

[48] PIERRE J-luc: Apports partiels d'actif, Revue de Droit Fiscal, n° 15-16, année 1999, page 607.

[49] Definition removed from Le Petit Larousse dictionary, Paris, 1993.

[50] RENAULT Olivier: Les nouveaux contours de la notion de branche complète et autonome d'activité, La Semaine Juridique Entreprises et Affaires, n°8-9 of February 21, 2002, page365.

transferring company. A branch is said to be autonomous with regard to the sector of activity if the product manufactured does not depend on the other production units of the transferring company.

The industry contains assets and liabilities: the industry is a set of assets and liabilities capable of operating autonomously. In this definition, the authors emphasize the need for both assets and liabilities to be present for a branch of activity to be considered autonomous.

In general, a company must have fixed assets, equipment and inventory from which to manufacture its commercial product. In most cases, these elements can be financed by loans, supplier debts or bank advances. In this case, the branch of activity is defined as an autonomous and independent unit. This independence implies the existence of the branch's own assets and liabilities, or those made available to the branch to enable it to fulfill its role of producing goods and services which, in turn, form part of the firm's overall production chain, as in the case of a packaging production unit belonging to a company producing television sets. In fact, it's a miniature of a company.

A partial contribution of assets involving the contribution of an autonomous branch of activity, and which may be subject to the preferential tax regime for mergers, must present similarities with other restructuring operations, namely mergers and demergers.

(B) Similarities between partial contributions, demergers and mergers :

In order to extract the similarities between the various restructuring operations, we will study the partial asset contribution and merger on the one hand, and the partial asset contribution and demerger on the other.

Merger and partial contribution of assets: a merger, as defined by article 411 of the CSC, "is the bringing together of two or more companies to form a single company. The merger may result either from the absorption by one or more companies of the other companies, or from the creation of a new company out of them".

A merger involves bringing together two or more pre-existing companies:

- Or they merge to form a single company through a merger or combination;
- Or one of them absorbs the others through a merger-absorption transaction.

Indeed, according to paragraph 2 of article 411 of the CSC, the merger results in the dissolution of the merged or absorbed companies and *the universal transfer of* their assets and liabilities to the new or absorbing company. This *dissolution does* not entail the liquidation of the merged or absorbed companies.

Thus, when one company absorbs another, the first increases its capital by means of a mixed contribution with assumption of liabilities, and the second, i.e. the absorbed company, decides on its early dissolution at the same time as the realization of its contribution.

According to the definitions set out in the Tunisian Commercial Code, a merger has two essential characteristics: the universal transmission of the assets of the absorbed company, and the dissolution of the latter as a result of the operation. But will these characteristics coincide with those of the partial contribution of assets?

As already defined, a partial contribution of assets is when a contributing company transfers part of its assets to a receiving company, with the aim of participating in the latter's share capital.

The company contributes part of its assets, rather than all of them, as is the case with the absorbed company in a merger; this explains why they are referred to as the contributing company and the absorbed company. On completion of a partial asset contribution, the contributing company retains the remainder of its assets and continues to exist, even carrying on its usual business. On the other hand, following a merger, the absorbed company no longer holds any assets and no longer exists: it is dissolved; this is the difference between a partial asset contribution and a merger.

Although the differences are remarkable, an analysis of these two operations, which are classified as corporate restructuring operations, reveals that they both involve an increase in capital. In the case of a partial contribution of assets, the beneficiary company records an increase in its share capital, while the absorbing or newly-created company will record the same operation, or even a constitution of this capital for the new company.

In addition, article 409 of the CCC requires certain objectives to be achieved through corporate restructuring operations, such as :

- development of working and distribution resources;
- increasing export capacity and competitiveness

-the realization of a capital base enabling greater investment, employment and productivity.

Merger and partial contribution of assets Although these two operations may seem very different, they are similar from the point of view of their objective.

Demerger and partial contribution of assets: According to article 428 of the CSC, a company is demerged by dividing its assets and liabilities between several existing companies or by creating new companies.

According to the accounting dictionary, the demerger of a company is its break-up by the contribution of all its assets and liabilities to new companies (outright demerger) or participation with them in the formation of new companies (merger-demerger by combination)[51] .

According to these two definitions, a demerger involves the transfer of all the assets and liabilities of the demerged company to pre-existing or new companies. The result is the dissolution without liquidation of the demerged company. However, it now seems that there are two types of demerger: total and partial. This is what we learn from article 428 of the CSC.

In reality, a partial demerger is no more than a partial contribution of assets, as defined above. The partial contribution may relate to one or more isolated items (e.g., a building or portfolio securities)

---

[51] Dictionnaire de comptabilité, éditions publications fiduciaires, Paris 2001, France.

or to a group of assets (e.g., the assets and liabilities of a given branch of activity).

The contribution of a branch of activity is comparable to a merger or demerger in terms of the assets contributed, with the difference that the partial contribution of assets does not result in the disappearance of the contributing company.

As already mentioned, a partial contribution may consist of :

- a transfer of a fraction of the assets of one company to another,
- a transfer of a complete branch of activity comprising both assets and liabilities.

Article 428 of the CSC therefore qualifies the second case as a partial demerger. Unlike a full demerger, a partial demerger does not result in the dissolution of the demerged company. In return for its contribution, the latter receives new shares created as a capital increase by the transferee company.

By qualifying the partial contribution of an autonomous and complete branch of activity as a partial demerger, the provisions of the articles of the CCC dealing with demergers are transposable to the partial contribution of assets.

Indeed, by considering the demerger as a merger, it benefits from the same substitution regime applicable to mergers. Given that the Tunisian legislator has not defined the tax treatment of the partial contribution, and has implicitly substituted the demerger for the merger within the framework of the tax regime. Assuming that the partial asset contribution of an autonomous branch is a partial demerger, it would be legitimate to subject it to the special merger regime. In fact, accepting that the partial contribution is a partial demerger is still insufficient to make it subject to the special merger regime. Other conditions must also be met.

§2: Conditions of access to the preferential regime

To benefit from the preferential merger regime, the partial contribution of assets relating to an autonomous branch of activity must meet other conditions.

Although the Tunisian legislator has omitted both the commercial and fiscal legal analysis, jurists have tried to settle the issue. Indeed, they have considered the partial contribution of assets to be a partial demerger. The tax authorities, for their part, are not as precise about the conditions for access to this regime. The partial demerger criterion alone is sufficient. With reference to French tax law, it should be noted that there are other conditions which may be transposable to Tunisia. In fact, if the contribution does not concern an autonomous branch of activity, i.e. a universal transfer of all the branch's assets and liabilities (A), ministerial approval is required to complete the operation (B).

(A) Universal transfer of branch assets :

A branch of activity is said to be autonomous if it contains assets and liabilities that can function together to produce goods and services.

When a partial transfer of assets takes place, the transferring company must transfer all its assets and liabilities to the receiving company, in order to benefit automatically from the preferential merger regime.

The transfer is said to be universal when it concerns all the assets and liabilities of the transferred branch. This transfer takes place automatically on completion of the contribution. In fact, a transfer is said to be universal when all the elements relating to the branch of activity are transferred. However, the partial contribution of assets relating to an autonomous branch of activity remains, despite its autonomy, part of a company known as the contributor. In this respect, the branch of activity may manage some of the transferring company's fixed assets, without being the owner. On completion of the contribution, the transferring company will only be able to transfer those assets that actually belong to the branch of activity.

The transferring company must respect the concept of universal transmission, with reference to a decision of the European Court of Justice (ECJ) handed down on January 15, 2002 concerning a partial asset contribution transaction carried out by a Danish company to a newly created company. The Danish company had misinterpreted the provisions of Directive 90/434 defining the concept of partial transfer of assets, and had therefore wished to retain part of the proceeds of the loan taken out before the transfer, the costs of which it had decided to transfer to the transferee company. In this case, the ECJ's decision was clear: this transfer was rejected, as it did not comply with the classic definition put forward by this directive: when a transaction provides for the retention, in the transferring company, of the proceeds of a major loan contracted by the latter and the transfer to the transferee company of the related obligations, there will be no partial transfer of assets within the meaning of article 2 of the[52] directive.

To be considered as a partial transfer of assets within the meaning of the directive, the transfer must relate to one or more autonomous branches of activity in their entirety, i.e. comprising all their assets and liabilities.

If the contribution does not concern a complete branch of activity, the transferring company must apply for ministerial approval to benefit from the special merger regime.

(B) Ministerial approval :

The partial contribution of assets may relate to one or more assets of the contributing company. However, the contribution may be a complete branch of activity, the characteristics of which were

---

[52] VERGEAT- EPESSON Béatrice : Dir n°90/434/CEE, July 23, 1990, régime fiscal des restructurations : notion d'apport partiel d'actifs, compétence de la cours, La Semaine Juridique Entreprise et Affaires n°2 du 9 janvier 2003, page 76.

studied above. The adoption of the contribution project in the case of one or more assets differs from that of an entire production unit. In the latter case, completion is automatic and emanates from the will of the parties. In the first case, on the other hand, the project is subject to ministerial approval. In fact, the concept of an autonomous branch of activity is referred to as a "passport to exemption from approval[53] ".

Under Tunisian law, partial asset contributions do not require ministerial approval. However, the Tunisian tax authorities do require formalities to be completed in the same way as for other restructuring operations, namely mergers and demergers.

In addition to obtaining ministerial approval, the transferring company must undertake to hold the shares acquired as consideration for the contribution for a certain period, as defined by both Tunisian and French legislation.

Once the conditions have been met, the partial asset contribution may be subject to the special merger regime.

Section II: Partial contributions subject to preferential merger treatment

The partial contribution of assets relating to an entire production unit, also known as an autonomous branch of activity, can benefit from the special merger regime. Given that the contribution of an autonomous branch of activity is considered a partial demerger, and that the Commercial Companies Code allows demerger transactions to adopt the tax rules of a merger, it would be logical to allow the partial contribution to adopt the rules of a merger. It would be logical to allow the partial contribution to adopt the merger rules.

Thus, the situation created by the partial transfer of assets of an autonomous branch of activity corresponds to an implicit adoption of the tax regime applicable to merger transactions.

Having approved the proposed partial transfer of assets, we need to examine the tax implications of this transfer. The transfer will cover all the assets and liabilities of the branch of activity.

The implications of the transaction, their tax treatment, and the precautions that should be taken, especially for tax auditors who may be called upon to examine this situation as part of their audit mission, will be presented in terms of corporate income tax, value-added tax and registration duties.

§1: At the level of the transferring company

The adoption of the partial asset contribution project has corporate tax implications. Once the taxable assets have been determined by the transferring company, it will be obliged to calculate its

---

[53] CASIMIR J-Pierre and CHDEFAUX Martial : apport partiel d'actif et branche complète d'activité ou la difficulté d'obtenir un passeport pour la dispense d'agrément, Revue Française de Comptabilité n°291, July-August 1997, page31.

taxable profit, which will be the sum of all income less deductible expenses. A deductible expense is any expense whose purpose is related to the usual operation of the company, whose amount is reasonable and whose justification exists.

In this case, the corporate income tax implications of the transaction concern both the transferring company and the receiving company.

(A) Direct taxes :

The Tunisian legislator has had the merit of regulating mergers and demergers much more than partial asset contributions, because Tunisian companies are small and medium-sized enterprises, and the most common transactions on the market are mergers and demergers. Given the legal vacuum surrounding partial asset contributions, we had to try and find a solution. In fact, the partial contribution of an autonomous branch of activity is considered by legal experts to be a partial demerger. Whether partial or total, a demerger borrows the tax rules of a merger, so that the partial contribution of assets relating to an autonomous and complete branch of activity also borrows the tax rules of a merger, and will therefore be treated in the same way as a merger. The Tunisian legislator has had the merit of regulating mergers and demergers much more than partial asset contributions, because Tunisian companies are small and medium-sized enterprises, and the most common transactions on the market are mergers and demergers.

At the level of the transferring company, it is necessary to study the effect of the transfer of the elements of the contribution in terms of direct tax.

capital gain on the contribution: Given that the partial contribution of assets relating to an autonomous branch of activity will be implicitly subject to the special merger regime under Tunisian law, it is logical to refer to the provisions governing merger operations.

With regard to capital gains on contributed assets, under article 48 of the Personal Income Tax Code and the Corporate Income Tax Code[54] , capital gains arising on the merger of companies are deductible from taxable profits.

In this case, the partial contribution of assets subject to the merger regime is governed by the same articles as mergers and demergers.

In this respect, article 48 of the aforementioned code applies to partial asset contribution transactions, and the capital gain remains exempt and is deducted from the taxable profit of the contributing company.

In addition, the exemption of this capital gain is subject to conditions for mergers, demergers and partial contributions of assets:

---

[54] Article 84, paragraph VII septies: "For the purposes of determining taxable profit, capital gains arising on the contribution, in the event of a company merger, of assets other than goods, property and securities used in the business are deductible".

- This capital gain must be realized on the assets contributed to the capital of the beneficiary company;

- The shareholders of the contributing company receive only shares in exchange for the contribution;

- Capital gains do not have to be derived from goods, as the goods and assets used in the business are[55].

"It follows that, from now on, the taxation of capital gains, whether total or partial, during or at the end of operations, constitutes the general principle, whereas the deduction of said capital gains from the taxable base constitutes the exception to this principle[56] ".

However, this derogation was adopted to encourage corporate restructuring operations, and the partial contribution of assets is one such operation. Article 50 of the said law now cites the case of mergers, and the partial contribution of assets as well as the demerger have certain similarities with the merger, with the tax authorities granting this privilege for any total or partial disposal, without even specifying whether the consideration will be equity securities or a sum of money. In fact, by referring to the definitions of restructuring operations, the consideration will be equity securities held by the transferring company. Moreover, since the conditions are also met by the partial contribution of assets, which is a set of assets and liabilities in exchange for equity securities, the justification for granting this privilege to the partial contribution of assets seems legitimate.

Going a little further in the same joint memo, the Director of the Tunisian General Tax Directorate contradicts himself, starting from the merger operation, which is characterized by the dissolution of the absorbed or contributing company of all its assets, he considers that the partial contribution of assets, which is characterized by the continuity of the contributing company, is a partial merger, and defines it as being the incorporation of autonomous economic entities.

"For tax purposes, the partial merger is considered as a partial disposal of assets and does not give rise to any particular advantage[57] .

The partial contribution of assets is not a partial disposal of assets, but the contribution of an autonomous branch of activity in exchange for equity interests. French authors do not consider a partial contribution to be a partial merger, but rather a partial cessation of activity by a company known as the contributor, which does not result in the disappearance of the contributing company.

Hence the contribution of an autonomous branch of activity is a partial demerger subject to the preferential capital gains regime for mergers, contrary to the second interpretation of the tax authorities.

---

[55] Note Commune N°34/98 commenting on article 50 of law n°97-88 of December 29, 1997 on the 1998 finance law, which extended the deduction from the corporate income tax base of capital gains on mergers of assets other than goods, property and securities used in the business.
[56] Idem.
[57] Ibidem

In addition to the three conditions already mentioned, both companies must be liable for corporate income tax. This condition seems questionable in the context of a partial asset contribution. The Tunisian legislator has neither defined the operation nor outlined its legal framework with any precision.

Legal entities as defined by the French corporate income tax code, i.e. corporations and limited liability companies, are subject to corporate income tax. General partnerships are subject to personal income tax. The tax will be paid by the partners in proportion to their stakes.

The partial contribution of assets concerns a set of assets and liabilities, or even a branch of activity. This type of operation is difficult to set up in the context of family partnerships, which are small businesses.

In the case of a limited liability company (société à responsabilité limitée) subject to corporate income tax, this operation is possible because the size is greater than in the first case.

By combining the management structure and the size of the company, the last condition will be verified in the context of a partial asset contribution transaction.

   * *Deferred losses and amortization*: In the context of mergers, losses generated by the operations of the absorbed company that could not be absorbed in the merger year are not transferred to the absorbing company, since the loss is linked to an operation. It can only be charged to the same operation, i.e. the one that incurred it.

The partial transfer of an autonomous branch of activity does not oblige the transferring company to change its business. Although the branch is autonomous, it belongs to a company whose activity depends on that of the branch, so the loss-making results of the branch will have to be offset against those of the transferring company. Any deferred depreciation not deducted from the results for the year in which the transaction took place will be lost by the transferring company.

(B) Registration duty and VAT :

The transferring company has no obligations with regard to registration, stamp duty or VAT.

§2: At the beneficiary company level :

Unlike the transferring company, the receiving company has other tax obligations that differ from those of the transferring company.

At the level of the beneficiary company, the transaction does not generate any taxable profit.

(A) Direct taxes :

At the level of the transferee company, depreciation of the assets transferred will be recognized, calculated on the basis of the net book value of the assets transferred or the legally revalued value.

(B) Registration duty and VAT:

Given that the tax consequences arising from the application of the normal regime are very onerous for the transferee company, and in order to compensate for this shortcoming, the legislator has provided for the application of a preferential regime with the aim of encouraging and inciting companies to adopt restructuring operations.

Indeed, in accordance with the provisions of article 23 of the registration and stamp duty code, the benefit of the preferential regime depends on the status of the person.

In other words, these companies must be set up in the form of a société anonyme, a société en commandite par action, a société à responsabilité limitée or a société coopérative, which means that partnerships, for example, cannot claim the benefit of this preferential regime.

The aforementioned article 23 specifies that the advantage in question consists of an exemption from the proportional transfer duty normally payable on all or part of the liabilities of the company or companies involved in the transaction.

This assumption of responsibility only gives rise to a fixed duty of 100 dinars on the deed recording it.

With regard to VAT, article 9-VI-4 of the VAT code stipulates that "in the event of a merger, amalgamation or transformation of the legal form of a company, the tax or the rel iquat of value-added tax paid in respect of goods and values giving entitlement to deduction, is transferred to the new company".

The transfer of this residue depends on whether the beneficiary company is a taxable company, a partial taxable company or even a non-taxable company.

In cases where the recipient company is not a taxable person and the transferring company is a taxable person, in accordance with the provisions of Article 9-VI-2 of the VAT Code[58] , the transferring company that is a taxable person is required to invoice the recipient company for the balance of VAT initially deducted and not acquired, and to pay it to the Treasury.

This adjustment consists of a repayment of the same amount of VAT deducted or which should have been paid or refunded, less one-fifth or one-tenth per year or fraction of a year of ownership, depending on whether the goods are capital goods or buildings.

In addition, when the beneficiary company is a partial VAT taxpayer, it benefits from the transfer of the residual value-added tax according to the pro rata rule[59] . The principle of earmarking can be

---

[58] Article 9-VI paragraph 2: "In the event of the sale, contribution to a company or change of use of these assets, or in the event of the cessation or abandonment of taxable status, a repayment must be made equal to the amount of value-added tax deducted or which should have been paid or refunded, less one-fifth per calendar year or fraction of a calendar year of ownership in the case of capital goods or equipment, and one-tenth per calendar year or fraction of a calendar year of ownership in the case of buildings. "

[59] Pro rata rule: P= (local sales incl. VAT+ export sales and similar incl. VAT+ suspended sales incl. VAT)/ (

applied when the organization of the beneficiary company allows it. In this case, the regulation only concerns the remainder that is supposed to serve the activity that is not subject to VAT, and will be invoiced.

Lastly, if the transferee company is subject to VAT, the balance of the tax paid on the deductible assets is transferred to the transferee company, enabling the latter to take the place of the transferring company in respect of the balance of deductible VAT. For the transferring company, this avoids having to pay back the tax to the treasury and invoice the recipient company for the amount of VAT to be regularized.

Chapter 2: The economic and tax benefits of adopting a special regime

"Every company undergoes transformations as a result of its active presence[60] . Tunisian companies, like any other, consider transformations throughout their lifespan, whatever the size and nature of their business. Economically, this transformation is said to be one form of strategic alliance among others.

These transformation operations generally have an economic rather than a fiscal or legal objective. Generally speaking, all strategic alliances are part of an industrial or commercial cooperation. Strategic alliances have three main objectives:

* transfer or acquire a new skill
* transfer or acquire identified know-how
* transfer or acquire an industrial, commercial or financial specialty.

The partial contribution of assets is one of the most effective ways of transforming a company. Following the adoption of the partial asset contribution transaction, the contributing company will have to record the partial cessation of the branch of activity contributed, and the amount of equity securities granted as a result of this transaction. For the transferee company, a capital increase must be recorded, which may lead to changes in the company's structure, necessitating amendments to the bylaws. In addition, the partial contribution of assets may be one of the objectives of strategic alliances and modification operations.

The decision to adopt a partial asset contribution is not an arbitrary one, and entrepreneurs cannot make random choices that could jeopardize their financial and managerial assets. The economic interest of adopting the partial contribution of assets, and the preference of entrepreneurs for this type of operation over mergers and demergers, is justified (section I).

In general, entrepreneurs often seek out businesses that offer the greatest possible tax

---

numerator + exempt sales + sales outside the scope of VAT).
[60]LAVALETTE Georges & NICULESCU Maria: Les stratégies de croissance, Paris, Editions d'Organisation 1999, page 285.

advantages. In some cases, they even tend to transfer their activities to locations that qualify as tax havens, for the same purpose.

The partial asset contribution operation, as already announced, has a dual system. As it is subject to the preferential merger regime, the partial contribution of assets offers a number of privileges to entrepreneurs, especially those with a long-term objective following the adoption of the contribution project. Mergers, demergers and partial contributions of assets are restructuring operations with more or less identical advantages, but the difference between the three lies in the material importance of each and the legal consequences of adopting one of them.

According to the Tunisian and French tax authorities, the partial contribution of assets relating to an autonomous branch of activity is subject to the preferential tax regime for mergers, and will therefore receive appropriate tax treatment. This treatment is advantageous for entrepreneurs, encouraging them to adopt this economic restructuring operation and not others.

To this end, the tax benefits of a partial transfer of assets are considerable in relation to its economic benefits (section II).

Section I: The economic benefits of adopting partial asset contributions

Being competitive is every manager's concern. Entrepreneurs are generally risk-takers, but the level of risk must not be too high. In the world of business, you have to be both risk-averse and risk-loving, and the manager is obliged to carry out a global but very precise study of his project before adopting it. The project study is the most important step in the business world. Some entrepreneurs entrust this task to specialized firms for fear of making mistakes themselves, while others prefer to carry out their own studies, even analyzing several perspectives to choose the best one.

Once the study has been carried out, the choice will be between one of the restructuring operations most suited to the firm's strategic policy, in order to improve its competitiveness (§1). Moreover, entrepreneurs may have a different view of the situation: some find that adopting one of the restructuring operations serves to improve competitiveness, while others are convinced by the fact that restructuring operations are forms of inter-firm partnership (§2).

§1 : Improving firm competitiveness :

Competitiveness is the goal and purpose of every economic project. The efficient combination of means of production and the careful choice of project contribute directly to improving a company's competitiveness. The partial transfer of assets is, on the one hand, one of a number of restructuring operations designed to mitigate the competition that seems increasingly fierce in a highly developed economic era. On the other hand, the partial contribution of assets is an investment choice by the recipient company. In fact, a study of the adoption of the contribution project is established before the actual adoption of the operation to detect the advantages and disadvantages of this investment choice in order to be able to manage.

(A) Restructuring operations and company competitiveness :

Since the promulgation of the Commercial Companies Code in November 2000, company mergers and similar operations have been governed by an appropriate legal framework.

These regulations are part of the government's reform policy, which has been underway for several years, to enable Tunisia to gradually integrate into the global economy. Indeed, the opening up of our borders to the outside world and the intensification of competition are forcing our companies to restructure if they are to survive. These include, of course, the phenomenon of concentration, which constitutes a veritable evolutionary process for our companies.

Under article 409 of the French Commercial Code, companies must pursue one of the following objectives when merging, in particular through mergers, demergers and partial asset contributions:

- adapting to internal and international economic change;
- the realization of a capital base enabling greater investment, employment and productivity;
- development of working and distribution resources;
- acquiring new technologies and improving product quality;
- increasing export capacity and competitiveness;
- strengthening the company's credibility with its partners;
- creating and strengthening jobs.

These objectives are all aimed, directly or indirectly, at making companies more competitive. This competitiveness can be both national and international. On the one hand, restructuring operations adopted by companies must pursue one of the aforementioned objectives. On the other hand, these restructuring operations themselves serve to improve the firm's competitiveness. By adopting one of the three restructuring operations, the pre-existing or newly-created beneficiary company will own assets, or even a set of assets, capable of operating autonomously. To this end, the choice of one of the operations is made by the two parties, i.e. the transferring company and the receiving company, and is most suited to their common needs and objectives.

Through the partial contribution of assets, the contributing and receiving companies are seeking, on the one hand, the survival of the contributing company, which is transferring only part of its assets, i.e. the autonomous branch of activity, and, on the other hand, the receiving company, which is considering a capital increase in line with its needs and easily adaptable to its former means of production.

Tunisian companies are generally small and medium-sized enterprises with an original capital structure in relation to their size. Admittedly, our companies are modest in size, but they choose between mergers, demergers and partial asset contributions to improve their production and be more competitive on the world market. In fact, these operations were only perfected with the promulgation of the Commercial Companies Code in November 2000. This regulation is justified by the development of trade and industry, and the increasing openness of the world market. However, as we have already mentioned, the Code only deals with mergers and demergers, and the legislator was a little cautious about partial asset contributions, simply listing them among the modalities without defining them.

In fact, the partial contribution of assets, whether explicitly or implicitly defined, is a restructuring operation used by companies much more than mergers and demergers, because it can adopt the tax privileges of a merger without obliging the contributing company to initiate a dissolution procedure. In addition to being a restructuring operation, is the partial contribution of assets nothing other than an investment choice?

(B) Partial contribution of assets: an investment choice :

From an industrial perspective, the company is an instrument for producing products and services. From an economic point of view, its function is to create wealth and added value. From a financial perspective, it's an investment opportunity. The objective of any firm is to make a profit on capital by minimizing risk, or more precisely, to opt for a solution offering a satisfactory risk/return ratio.

To achieve this objective, the company looks for all possible means. Recourse to shareholders for an ordinary capital increase can be seen as an ordinary solution, but if self-financing does not meet the partners' or shareholders' objective, external financing should be sought.

Recourse to the bank is the company's first refuge when it comes to increasing its capital, but this solution can sometimes prove difficult to implement, as the bank demands guarantees that the company is not in a position to provide. To this end, the company will have to look for other terms and conditions, or make investments that will enable it to achieve its objective directly. Leasing may appear to be the ideal solution, but it may be fraught with other difficulties, such as finding the right personnel to operate the acquired equipment, integrating the new equipment into the company's production process, and paying the costs associated with the leased equipment.

To avoid all these problems, it is in the company's interest to choose one of the following restructuring operations: merger, demerger or partial contribution of assets. The choice of one of these operations depends on the strategic decision. As with any investment decision, the choice of one or other of the restructuring operations must go through the necessary stages to judge the possible results of such a choice.

For some companies, the partial contribution of assets, i.e. a production unit capable of operating by its own means, appears to be the most appropriate investment choice. It offers the advantage of investing at zero cost. In fact, the transferee company will not have to pay a sum of money to the transferring company. In return, the contributing company will receive equity securities. As a result of this operation, the capital of the receiving company increases. In this way, the recipient company realizes the partial asset contribution as an investment choice.

But why do companies prefer partial asset contributions?

§2: The strategic preference for inter-firm partnerships :

Partnership is a form of cooperation between two or more firms with the aim of improving the competitiveness of one of the participating firms.

Faced with increasingly fierce competition, Tunisian companies need to be more competitive. Tunisia's openness to the global economy is forcing Tunisian firms to improve their competitiveness if they are to withstand the economic pressure of the multinationals they face.

To achieve this, Tunisian small and medium-sized companies need to cooperate with each other, or even merge, to reach the size and production capacity needed to keep up with the giants.

The partial contribution of assets is one way of achieving this objective. But will entrepreneurs really use this restructuring operation as a means of cooperation (A) or as a control technique (B)?

(A) Partial contribution of assets: a means of cooperation :

In the world of economics, unity creates strength. That said, Tunisian companies, like all others, are obliged to work together to produce goods and services that meet world standards, and have done so since Tunisia joined the GATT agreement.

As we have already seen, the partial contribution of assets is a convincing investment choice for Tunisian companies with such a particular structure in terms of size.

Tunisian companies, classified as small and medium-sized enterprises, are unable to compete with the giant corporations that hold the lion's share of the world market. As a result, our Tunisian entrepreneurs are using economic restructuring operations to meet the needs of this market.

Mergers and demergers enable companies to group together and achieve a size comparable to that of international competitors, thus enabling them to produce at a level similar to that of their competitors in terms of quantity.

On the other hand, the union of means of production enables companies to improve their production quality so that it can reach the production level of multinationals.

The partial contribution of assets is a special form of inter-company cooperation. The contributing company participates with a branch of activity that will serve to improve the productivity of that firm.

The two companies, the contributor and the beneficiary, will be bound by the contribution. The contributor will be a shareholder in proportion to its stake, and will be entitled to participate in the meetings of the beneficiary company.

For its part, the beneficiary company will own or even enjoy all or part of the autonomous branch of activity thus transferred.

On the face of it, the two companies have complementary motivations, although in reality they are antagonistic. The transferring company seeks to overvalue its contribution in order to gain the largest share in the capital of the receiving company, which for its part seeks to have this contribution with the lowest possible value, so as not to cede a large part of its capital to a company which may subsequently become a shareholder exercising its power for its own personal benefit.

(B) Partial contribution of assets: a control technique :

When it comes to corporate auditing and control, a company's shareholders can exercise three types of control:

- exclusive control ;
- joint control ;
- significant influence.

These three types of control are different from one another, and a shareholder may exercise one of them depending on his or her stake in the company's capital.

A shareholder is any individual or legal entity holding a portion of a company's capital in return for a contribution advanced by the company.

In the business world, cross-holdings between different companies are just as common. This cross-fertilization of capital creates a certain complementarity and dependence between the companies involved.

A priori, this cross-shareholding stems from a desire to cooperate, but an analysis of certain shareholdings in Tunisian companies reveals that these operations are essentially adopted with the aim of carrying out one of the aforementioned forms of control. This type of operation is adopted by companies operating in the same business sector. At the beginning of the 1980s, *Zaoui meubles* adopted a project for the partial contribution of assets, known at the time as a merger or partial demerger, to *Skanes meubles, with the* aim of specializing in the manufacture of a single category of household furniture. The beneficiary company, *Skanes meubles,* having completed the transfer of the production unit contributed by *Zaoui meubles*, began to exercise its power of exclusive control over the contributing company, while adopting strategic decisions favorable to it.

Given that the beneficiary company exercised its control in accordance with the rules while being the majority shareholder in the capital of the contributing company, the latter ended up being absorbed by *Skanes meubles*, which bankrupted it.

The partial contribution of assets is therefore an effective tool for inter-company control, as it enables the contributing company to gain access to the capital of the beneficiary company with a lower risk of failure, especially if the beneficiary company is already in existence.

Section II: The tax benefits of adopting the proposed partial asset contribution :

As already announced, the adoption of the partial contribution of assets is in the interest of both the contributing and the beneficiary companies. Classified as an economic restructuring operation, the partial contribution of assets proves its frequent adoption by both Tunisian and foreign companies.

In fact, the preference for the partial asset contribution transaction over the merger or demerger is justified by the convenience of this transaction, which allows the survival of the transferring company, and the possibility of subjecting this transaction to the preferential merger regime. In this respect, the partial asset contribution operation borrows the advantages of the merger and demerger while retaining its specificity.

Generally, when a given operation is found to be advantageous for economic development, the legislator gives it a legal incentive to further encourage companies to adopt it, as is the case with the partial contribution of assets.

However, the importance of this operation and its increasingly frequent use have prompted legal experts and the Tunisian tax authorities to find a special treatment for this type of operation, while maintaining its attractiveness for the restructuring and transformation of Tunisian companies.

This vision of Tunisian administrative doctrine has above all focused attention on the tax advantages of a partial contribution of assets transaction involving an autonomous branch of activity, in cases where it is subject to the preferential merger regime.

However, this interest is misinterpreted by our entrepreneurs, who divert the objective of adopting this restructuring operation. As a tax-privileged option, the partial contribution of assets is the choice of most managers, who tend to reduce or even eliminate their tax burden, even through the adoption of a fictitious partial contribution.

§1: Virtually tax-neutral partial asset contributions :

For tax purposes, taxable income is the sum of categorical income and deductible expenses. The adoption of the partial contribution of assets will result in the transfer of the elements of the branch of activity from the contributing company to the beneficiary company. The consequences of this transfer are purely tax-related. As already discussed in Part 1, the transferring company is involved in a revalued branch of activity, in order to extract its current value, which in most cases exceeds its historical cost. From a tax point of view, the revaluation of an asset or group of assets generates a capital gain or loss, taxable or exempt depending on the circumstances. The capital gain or loss arising from the partial transfer of assets is the main consequence of the transfer of the components of the branch of activity transferred. Based on French tax law, the legislator considers that the partial contribution of assets has a dual system. The contribution of an autonomous branch of activity enables this transaction to be subject to the preferential merger regime, whereas otherwise the partial contribution is a simple transfer of assets subject to the ordinary tax regime. However, in return for its contribution, the contributing company receives shares in the capital of the beneficiary company, which excludes the notion of transfer of assets from the transaction. Unlike a merger, which results in the disappearance of the absorbed company, the contributing company survives the partial asset contribution. What's more, following a merger operation, the amount of the merger result is estimated to be very significant, provided that an entire company disappears. Unlike a merger, not only does the transferring company survive, but the branch of activity transferred is replaced by a certain number of shares. There will be no actual cash inflow, and in accordance with the principle of prudence and the accounting convention of linking expenses to income, the consideration for the partial contribution of assets cannot constitute income. Being a shareholder in a company does not guarantee a profit for future years. A shareholder is a natural or legal person who benefits from the profit and bears the loss with his or her co-partners or co-shareholders.

The partial transfer of assets transaction is a simple transfer of a set of assets in exchange for shares in the company. In fact, the capital gain generated by this transaction will not be distributed to the shareholders. Hence, it seems pointless to subject the partial asset contribution to the preferential merger regime. Similarly, there is no convincing justification for taxing the capital gain on the grounds that the partial transfer of assets is a simple transfer of the assets of the transferring company. As already mentioned, this transaction does not meet the necessary conditions to qualify as a sale, especially if the transferring company does not intend to sell the shares acquired as a result of this transaction.

At the level of the receiving company, the transfer of the elements of the autonomous branch of activity will have other consequences. The transferred branch of activity includes fixed assets which must be registered. To this end, the transferee company must register the fixed assets and all contracts relating to the transaction. In addition, the receiving company will have to record an increase in capital, which is subject to special registration. On the recipient company's side, whether the partial asset contribution transaction is subject to the ordinary law regime or to the merger regime, the necessary registration is required.

On the recipient company's side, the partial asset contribution transaction does not appear to be without tax consequences. This operation is not neutral on the part of the beneficiary company.

§2: Diversion from the purpose of the partial asset contribution transaction :

Considered among restructuring operations, the partial contribution of assets remains the preferred option for Tunisian entrepreneurs, because of the interest it presents.

The fact that this operation is subject to the preferential merger regime, which exempts the capital gain generated on the transfer of parts of the branch, and the survival of the transferring company, justify our entrepreneurs' preference for this investment choice.

In this way, the contribution of a complete and autonomous branch of activity sometimes enables the transferring company to get rid of the branch that was blocking the company's activity. If the transferring company goes through a temporary freeze, or even if it chooses to partially change its field of activity, it may choose to participate with the branch of activity concerned in the capital of another company operating in the same field, instead of selling this branch and subsequently being obliged to meet its tax obligations. In this case, the transferring company uses the partial asset contribution transaction to disguise the sale of a set of assets, thereby avoiding payment of the capital gains tax.

In addition, it has already been shown that the partial contribution of assets can be used as a means of control of one company by another, which can create conflicts between the partners of the beneficiary company, who risk being managed by the new partner, who in most cases is the majority shareholder.

Since the contribution of an autonomous branch of activity entitles the contributing company to a liquidation grace of the amount of the related capital gain, it can abuse this privilege with its accomplice, the beneficiary company, to set up a fictitious partial asset contribution transaction. Both parties can choose the most important branch of activity to set up their fictitious project.

General conclusion

One of the most important and widely used restructuring operations in the business world is the partial transfer of assets.

Restructuring is the only operation that has no legal definition. The Tunisian legislator has simply listed the operation as one of the ways of increasing the capital of an existing company or creating a new company. The French legislator, for its part, has dealt with the operation only incidentally.

Indeed, the importance of this operation in the life of a company and the ambiguity of its tax treatment under Tunisian law make this subject all the more important.

Under French law, the partial contribution of assets is governed by a dual system. It can either be assimilated to a contribution in kind, or be subject to the demerger regime.

The choice of one or other of these two assimilations depends, on the one hand, on the choice of the two parties and, on the other hand, on the nature of the elements making up the partial asset contribution.

By definition, a partial contribution concerns a set of assets and liabilities, or an autonomous branch of activity capable of operating by its own means. The two definitions are similar, but what makes the difference is the nature of the autonomous operation.

Whether the partial contribution of assets is treated as a contribution in kind or a demerger, its adoption is subject to a general procedure. This procedure is generally the same for all partial asset contributions, whether or not they are subject to the demerger regime.

The transfer of the elements of the partial asset contribution has tax consequences, but the omission or negligence of a description of the tax treatment of this operation.

This book analyses the tax treatment of the transaction, pointing out that there are not two possible regimes, but a standard regime for this transaction and another adapted treatment.

Indeed, accepting that the partial asset contribution is a simple contribution in kind requires certain steps similar to those adopted in the case where the partial asset contribution relates to a complete branch of activity and is therefore subject to the demerger regime.

The main effect of the completion of a partial contribution of assets is the transfer of the elements of the contribution. This transfer has a tax impact which is summarized in the calculation of the a priori taxable amount and the registration of all the elements of the contribution.

To calculate this taxable amount, a series of stages must be completed: valuation of the elements of the contribution, verification of the draft contribution and the value of the contribution by the contribution auditor, and approval of the draft contribution by the extraordinary general meeting or constituent assembly.

Once this taxable matter has been calculated, it will be necessary to deal with the common law regime governing partial asset contributions involving one or more of the transferring company's assets and liabilities. In addition, the partial contribution of an autonomous branch of activity is subject to special tax treatment. Tunisian tax law does not explicitly define the scope of this operation, but only considers it as part of a corporate restructuring. As a result, the partial contribution of assets, like demergers, is implicitly subject to the merger tax regime. However, having dealt with this submission, and with reference to both French and European law, it would appear that this submission is not conclusively justified by the differences between the two operations.

Throughout this work, which is essentially concerned with Tunisian law, we have made assimilations and comparisons, even indirect, with French law, in view of the fact that the subject does not even have a sufficiently explicit existence in tax matters.

Bibliography

Practical information :

Bulletin Joly Société; 1994 edition.

Dictionnaire RF Groupe Revue Fiduciaire, Fiscal, 18ième edition, 2003.

Dictionnaire Permanent Fiscal: Fusions, Scissions et Apports Partiels d'Actif; 1999 edition.

Dictionnaire Permanent Fiscal: Taxation of European Union member states; 1998 edition.

Edition Francis Lefebvre, Gestion Fiscale de l'entreprise; 2001 edition.

Edition Francis Lefebvre, La pratique des restructurations: Fusions, Scissions, Apports partiels d'actifs et opérations internationales; 2001 editions.

Jurisclasseur Sociétés; 1998 editions.

Jurisclasseur Fiscal; 1998 edition.

Lamy Commercial; 2003 edition.

Lamy Fiscal; 2003 edition.

Manuel permanent du droit des affaires; 2000-2001 Amamou law firm edition.

Manuel permanent du droit Fiscal et du Droit de Douane Tunisien ; édition cabinet Amamou janvier 1996.

Mémento pratique Francis Lefebvre, Fiscal 2003.

Mémento pratique Francis Lefebvre, Sociétés commerciales; 2002 edition.

Mémento pratique Francis Lefebvre, Concurrence Consommation; 2003-2004 edition.

Le Système Comptable des Entreprises, published by Imprimerie officielle de la République Tunisienne, 2002.

General works :

AYADI Habib : Droit fiscal : Impôt sur le revenu des personnes physiques et impôt sur les sociétés ; édition center d'études, de recherches et de publications, édition 2001.

CHADEFAUX M: Les fusions de sociétés; published by La Villeguerin; 1990.

COMMUNIER Jean-Michel: Droit fiscal communautaire; published by Bruylant Brussels, 2001.

COZIAN Maurice: Précis de fiscalité des entreprises, 26 edition Litec 2003.

COZIAN Maurice and VIANDIER Alain: Droit des sociétés 10 édition Litec 1997.

COZIAN Maurice , DEBOISSY Florence & VIANDIER Alain : Droit des sociétés , édition Litec juris classeur 15 édition 2002.

GUYON Yves: Droit des affaires T1, 9th edition, Economica 1996.

GOLIARD François: Droit fiscal des entreprises, published by LGDJ; 2002-2003.

LAVALETTE Georges & NICULESCU Maria: Les stratégies de croissances, éditions d'organisation; 1999.

LECLERCQ Christophe & Xavier: Gestion stratégique de la concurrence en temps de crise, published by Maxima; 1993.

LEGEAIS Dominique: Droit commercial des affaires, 13^{ieme} edition, Armand Colin 2000.

MERLE Philippe: Droit commercial, sociétés commerciales, 5ième edition, Dalloz;1997.

Q **OUDENOT Philippe**: Fiscalité approfondie des sociétés, Litec 2001.

RIPERT and ROBLOT by M. Germains: Traité du droit commercial, 16^{ieme} edition, LGDJ 1996.

SAINTOURENS Bernard: Le droit des affaires, Grenoble University Press, 1997.

ffl **TOURNIER J-Claude & J- Baptiste**: L' évaluation d'entreprise: que vaut une entreprise? éditions d'organisation 2001.

Specialized books :

Université Catholique de LOUVAIN, Centre d'études Jean RENAULD: Le nouveau droit des fusions et des scissions de sociétés (collective); Collection Droit des Sociétés, volume 5, 1994.

DINH Yanick: Les fusions, scissions et apports partiels d'actifs : Aspects comptables , juridiques et fiscaux, éditions ESKA; 2000.

Q **DE KERGOS Yann, RAFFIN Marie-Hélène & MARTIN Philippe**: Fiscalité des fusions et apports partiels d'actifs, Litec 1994.

Articles :

□ **Ben AMOR Hamadi**: Fusion, scission et apport partiel d'actif dans le cadre de la nouvelle législation. Revue Comptable et Financière tunisienne n°54, fourth quarter 2001, page 61.

□ **BEL HADJ BRAHIM Chédlia**: The opening up of the Tunisian economy to the Euro-Mediterranean area has had a considerable influence on the reform of our company law. sociétés, Revue de l'Entreprise n°51 January-February 2001, page 20.

□ **CHARTIER Yves** : apport partiel d'actif : Revue des Sociétés(l), Janvier- Mars 1997 page110.

□ **CHEOUR Nadia**: Fusions-acquisitions: Techniques d'évaluation d'une entreprise, Revue de l'Entreprise n°55 September-October 2001, page 7.

□ **CASIMIR Jean-Pierre** and **CHADEFAUX Martial** Apport partiel d'actif et branche complète d'activité ou la difficulté d'obtenir un passeport pour la dispense d'agrément : Revue Française de Comptabilité 291, July - August 1997, page 31.

- **DESLANDES Michel**: Fusion des sociétés- APA: Droit des Sociétés, February 1994 No. 42.

- **DIBOUT Patrick**: Le régime fiscal français des fusions et opérations assimilées sous la lumière de la directive du 23 juillet 1990, Revue de Droit Fiscal n°27 de l'année 2002.

- **FEKI Néjib** : La loi du 3 novembre 2000 constitue une refonte du droit des sociétés qui tient compte des impératifs dictés par l'environnement actuel de l'entreprise tunisienne ; Revue de l'Entreprise n°51 janvier-février 2001, page 23.

- **JUFFROY Marc**: Le processus des opérations de fusions et acquisitions : un rôle pour l'audit interne :Revue de l'Audit n°161 September 2002

- **KOLSI Samir** : Quelques réflexions sur les insuffisances du nouveau code des sociétés commerciales ; Revue de l'Entreprise, n°51 janvier-février 2001, page13

- **LE NABASQUE:** Apport partiel d'actif: Droit des Sociétés, February1993 (n°39, 40)

- **LE NABASQUE:** La soumission d'un apport partiel d'actif au régime des scissions dispense du respect des formalités de l'article 1690 du code civil, Droit des Sociétés, May 1994.

- **LE NABASQUE :**Expertise de gestion, l'APA est une opération de gestion s'il n'a pas été soumis au régime des scissions : Droit des Sociétés, March 1993 (No. 58).

- **LUCAS François-Xavier and VIDAL Dominique**: La responsabilité civile du commissaire aux comptes : Droit des Sociétés, April 2001.

- **MAMLOUK Amel** : L'apport du code des sociétés commerciales à la protection des créanciers par le capital social ; Revue de la jurisprudence et de la législation(tunisienne), édition du center d'études juridiques et judiciaires du ministère de justice, N°9, novembre 2001, page9.

- **MARTEAU-PETIT**: Sociétés par action, apport partiel d'actif d'une branche d'activité, effet : Droit des Sociétés, August-September 1991.

- **PIERRE Jean-Luc**: La plus-value de cession de droits sociaux et déficit catégoriel professionnel: Revue Droit des Sociétés, December 1999.

- **PIERRE Jean-Luc**: Application du régime spécial des fusions aux apports partiels d'actifs, Droit des Sociétés, May 2002.

- **RENAULT Olivier** : Les nouveaux contours de la notion de branche complète et autonome d'activité. La semaine juridique Entreprise et Affaires n°8 -9 of February 21, 2002.

- **SAINTOURENS Bernard**: Expertise de gestion: Revue des Sociétés.

- **SERLOOTEN Patrick:** Enregistrement, droits autres ceux frappant les mutations à titre gratuit, jurisclasseur fiscal 1993.

- **VIDAL Dominique**: Commissaire à la fusion responsabilité (no) : Company law

Sociétés, February 1999.

- **VILLEMOT Dominique**: Effet rétroactif ou différé des fusions scissions et apports partiels d'actifs, Revue de Droit Fiscal n°24 de l'année 2001.

- **VILLEMOT Dominique:** La nouvelle définition des fusions et des scissions, Revue de Droit Fiscal n°25 for 2002.

- **VILLEMOT Dominique :** Le régime fiscal de faveur des fusions et des apports partiels d'actifs : des précisions apportées, des interrogations qui subsistent, Revue de Droit Fiscal n°46 pour l'année 1993.

- **VILLMOT Dominique**: Le régime fiscal de faveur des fusions et des AP A: Droit Fiscal 1993 N° 46.

- **VILLMOT Dominique :** Les aménagements apportés au régime des apports partiels d'actifs et des scissions : des avancées incontestables qui doivent se poursuivre. Revue de Droit Fiscal n°36 for the year 2000.

Case law :

Cass Comm, January 12, 1993, Revue des Sociétés 1993, page 426, note by SAINTOURENS Bernard.

Cass Comm, February 16, 1988, Revue Trimestrielle de Droit Commercial 1988, page 639.

Cass Comm, June 4, 1996, Revue des Sociétés, January-March 1997, note by CHARTIER Yves.

CAA Paris, May 28, 1998, request no. 94-1916, Société Cocinor.

Thesis and Dissertations :

- **CHANTAING Jean-Michel :** L'apport partiel d'actif soumis au régime des fusions-scissions ou l'ambiguïté du renvoi contenu dans l'article 387 de la loi du 24 juillet 1966 ; thèse soutenue en novembre 1994 à l'Université Panthéon-Assas (PARIS II), sous la direction de SYNVET Hervé ; 246 pages.

- **ARBI Fatiha :** Les caractéristiques des techniques fiscales de transferts indirectss au sein des groupes de sociétés ; mémoire pour l'obtention du diplôme d'études approfondies en gestion, sous la direction de REZGUI Salah. 1992-1993, 146 pages.

- **AROUSSE Radhouane :** le commissaire aux apports : aspect juridiques et techniques de la mission ; mémoire de maîtrise Institut Supérieur de Gestion de Sousse 2000-2001 60 pages.

- **BOUAOIJA Souraya :** l'incorporation de l'apport en nature dans le capital social ; mémoire de maîtrise Institut Supérieur de Gestion Sousse 2000-2001 53 pages.

- **HASSINE Haifa**: Les scissions d'entreprises; dissertation for DESS Droit de l'entreprise Faculté des Sciences Juridiques, Politiques et Sociales de Tunis 1999-2000, 120 pages.

□ **OULED ABDELDAYEM Mohamed ouled Meïmine**: Les déterminants des fusions-acquisitions et le choix d'un mode d'intégration entre les structures des entreprises (cas de la Tunisie) ; mémoire pour l'obtention du diplôme d'études approfondies en sciences de gestion, under the supervision of FRIOUI Mohamed, 1998-1999. 233 pages.

Laws :

□ French law of 24-07-1966 relating to mergers and demergers.

□ Law n°2002-101 of December 17, 2002, on the 2003 Finance Act; JORT n°102, page 2875.

□ Loi du 29-07-1991 relative à la concurrence et au prix modifiée et complétée par la loi du 24-04-1995 ; JORT n° 55, page1393.

Conventions :

□ Convention Internationale entre la république Tunisienne et la république Française en vue d'éviter les doubles impositions en matière d'impôt sur le revenu et sur la fortune of May 28, 1973.

Guidelines :

□ European Community Council Directive no. 90/434/EEC of July 23, 1990, OJEC no. L 225, published on 20-08-1990, on the tax treatment of mergers, divisions, transfers of assets and exchanges of shares concerning companies of different Member States, since the Official Journal of the European Communities.

□ Bulletin Officiel des impôts, direction générale des impôts 4 I-2-02 N° 185 du 25 octobre 2002 : impôt sur les sociétés. Special provisions. Mergers and similar operations.

Codes :

□ Tunisian Commercial Code.

□ Tunisian Commercial Code.

□ Personal income tax and corporate income tax code.

□ Registration and stamp code.

□ VAT and consumer law code.

□ Code annoté des Droits d'Enregistrements et de Timbres for 2001.

□ French General Tax Code.

□ French Company Codes.

Common notes :

Note commune n°34/98; Bulletin officiel des douanes et des impôts, texte n°DGI 98/57.

Note commune n°6/2002; Bulletin officiel des douanes et des impôts, texte n°DGI 2002/15.